One American Must Die

One American Must Die

A Hostage's Personal Account of the Hijacking of Flight 847

Kurt Carlson

CONGDON & WEED

Published by Congdon & Weed, Inc.
298 Fifth Avenue, New York, New York 10001
Distributed by Contemporary Books, Inc.
180 North Michigan Avenue, Chicago, Illinois 60601
Manufactured in the United States of America

Published simultaneously in Canada by Beaverbooks, Ltd.
195 Allstate Parkway, Valleywood Business Park
Markham, Ontario L3R 4T8 Canada

Robert Dean Stethem
1961–1985

"The terrorists focused their brutality on a brave young man who was a member of the armed forces of the United States. . . . We will not forget what was done to him. There will be no forgetting. His murderers must be brought to justice."

President Ronald Reagan
Andrews Air Force Base
July 2, 1985

Contents

Acknowledgments

Without assistance from my family and office staff, one family's story of Flight 847 could not have been completed in the few months after my return. They pieced together the family crisis at home, and encouraged me to write my story as it happened, hour by hour, from beginning to end.

I thank my wife, Cheri; my parents, Ed and Vie Carlson; my brothers and sisters, Jan Waldner, Bun Carlson, Mark Carlson, Gini Kittle, and Edwin Carlson; my in-laws, Charlene and Marshall Strickland; and my "hostage" office staff, writers Joe Lamb and Chuck Sweeney and manager Martha Johnson.

I also extend my gratitude to Contemporary Books editor Libby McGreevy for her hard work and guidance.

One American Must Die

Prologue:
The Lebanese
A-Team

In the stifling heat of a basement cell in Beirut, Lebanon, five weary, bearded men huddled over an orange pocket radio tuned to a BBC newscast. They had been held prisoner in this cell for thirteen long days, carefully plotting to take matters into their own hands if all else failed.

The news from London was not good.

Ronald Reagan was saying he'd give the diplomats just three more days to gain the release of the hostages of TWA Flight 847. After that, he would consider "new measures" to resolve the crisis. The threat was clear.

"We have no choice," one of the five men said. "We have to be ready to make a run for it."

At almost the same moment, deep in the basement of the Nassau Colliseum in Uniondale, New York, a band of unlikely conspirators met to lay their own plan of action.

"We have people standing by with vehicles and weapons," the one with the dark eyes and olive complexion said. "They are prepared to storm the house where he is being held and take him out by force if that becomes necessary."

"Great," chortled the rock and roll drummer. "That's the best damned news I've had all week. If Reagan screws up, we go get him with our own commando squad. It's wild as can be, but it just might work."

1
Into the Vortex

Ladies and gentlemen, welcome aboard TWA Flight 847. . . ."

The sleek Boeing 727 was still climbing—my seat belt was still latched—when all hell broke loose.

Two men in white leisure suits and black shirts charged up the aisle, screaming, "Come to die! Americans die!"

One of them leaped into the air and dropkicked a flight attendant in the chest, slamming her hard against the bulkhead.

Both waved huge .45 automatics, and one fumbled with the safety pin of a pineapple-shaped hand grenade while the other pounded on the cockpit door.

I bolted upright in my seat, my blood running cold.

"God help us all," I prayed. I knew this was going to be a long, terrible trip.

I had not wanted to go.

I mean, I didn't want to be here in the first place. Maybe it was a premonition, maybe not—I don't know—but a lot of things about this trip had been unusual.

A week earlier, on Saturday morning, June 8, 1985, I had packed my bags, not exactly thrilled about my unexpected trip to Cairo, Egypt. I am a construction officer in the 416th Engineer Command, U.S. Army Reserve. My unit was involved in Operation Bright Star, a joint field exercise of U.S. and Egyptian armed forces. I was volunteered, Army style, for a one-week reconnaissance mission.

At my general's request, I was to join several other members of the Rapid Deployment Force (RDF) in meetings with the Egyptian military command. The RDF is an army within an army made up of select units from all branches of the service. Our planners were in a quandary. They didn't have enough logistical information for the exercise in August. Our people wanted to have things planned out well in advance of the exercise, but the Egyptians thought that wasn't enough like a real war. They wanted all plans coordinated just prior to the event.

The general said he needed someone who could work with people and get the job done. Besides being a good troubleshooter, I have a reputation for solving logistical problems. That means I have a knack for scrounging and cutting through red tape to find answers. Sometimes you have to improvise to get things done in the army.

I guess I've always been a pushover for the army. It's my other job, my hobby, my source of adventure. Once a month, I cruise into Chicago for weekend duty. For two weeks a year, I fly to some exotic country for training. At home in Rockford, Illinois, I am a roofing contractor.

As my departure day neared, my pride at being chosen to help straighten out the snafu and my desire for adventure were deflated.

Cairo? In June? It would be hot. Several years before, I had toured Egypt in February, and it was hot even then.

In addition, I had business concerns at home. My roofing business was cranking at full speed. I also was in the middle of developing an office and fitness park, where we had just started three new buildings. One of the buildings was a fitness center, to be managed by my wife, Cheri. She is both a businesswoman and an athlete, having placed in several national bodybuilding competitions.

But the real reason I wanted to stay home was only five months old: "Little Mac," we call her—Meredith Alice Carlson. Cheri and I had been married seventeen years before our little one was born. In addition to God, we could thank a Palestinian-American doctor who had emigrated from Beirut for making it possible for us to have our first child.

In a melancholy mood at the thought of leaving, I sat out by the pool, holding Meredith and studying her every move and expression. It was as if I might never see her again. Cheri joined us. She had tears in her eyes. Now that we were a family, these army trips were hard for her to bear.

"If it's going to be too much, I'll just cancel out. I'll call the army and say I'm staying home," I said.

"No, we'll be all right," Cheri said. "But one of these days you'll have to learn to say no to the army."

"Well, I should be able to finish up early, maybe in five or six days. I promise to be home by Friday. And next time I'll say no."

Cheri gave a wan smile. "You'll never change, but we love you anyway. Just remember Meredith and I need you more than the army needs you."

It was difficult, but I put aside my feelings and prepared to go.

In keeping with military travel procedures, I removed most of my identification and credit cards from my wallet, taking only my army ID card, driver's license, and one credit card. I was told to take my military health records, which would be needed should I become ill in Egypt. This precaution was necessary since I had no time to get all the vaccinations required by the army.

Dad picked me up around noon for the 90-minute drive to O'Hare International Airport. We talked business most of the way.

When we arrived at the airport, Dad whipped out a camera and took pictures of me standing on the sidewalk with my bags in hand.

I thought, "That's funny. Dad hasn't done this since I was a kid."

It was hot, and passengers crowded into the temporary international terminal. The city was building a new terminal, and the lines were unbearably long. It was just like the army—hurry up and wait.

I had a TWA round-trip Chicago-to-Cairo ticket. The army was worried about my getting through Egyptian customs because they didn't have time to get me a visa and draft my military orders. So I had to change my ticket to Pan Am, to join up with some of the other RDF men in New York. Apparently the army thought it would be easier to smuggle me in with the group. They also wanted to brief me during the flight about security and the correct "manners" to use in Egypt during the Muslim holy month, Ramadan.

As always seems to happen when you need a ticket rewrite, I got a ticket agent experiencing her first day on the job.

"Wouldn't it be better to fly Pan Am both ways?" she asked.

"Why not?" I replied and canceled my return trip on TWA. There was just one problem. The return Pan Am flight she booked me on, from Cairo to Rome, had been dropped two months before.

For me, her error would prove catastrophic.

In New York, I met Sergeant Major Robert Martin from RDF headquarters in Atlanta and Major Keith Wedge, a fellow officer with the 416th, who had flown in from St. Louis. Keith was our well-drilling engineer. He was concerned about finding pure water near the Bright Star site—a real problem in the desert.

The G-2 (security) briefing during the flight from New York was simple enough. "When you get to Cairo, don't say anything to anybody. They have tourist police everywhere, and they are all members of Egyptian Intelligence," Martin said.

Well, Intelligence people are the same everywhere, I thought, and if Egyptian Intelligence is telling their people, "Don't say anything to anybody," it will be difficult to get anything done.

Although I knew little about it, there's nothing super-secret about Operation Bright Star. The exercises are held every couple of years, and the whole thing is viewed by all sorts of military brass and government diplomats. For all I know, there are Soviet KGB agents in the crowd. They too had probably been told, "Don't say anything to anybody."

During the exercise, all the important officials sit on reviewing stands to watch the armies maneuver and blow up targets. Our navy links up with the Egyptians' to stage an amphibious landing. Our airborne units bring along a couple of howitzers and a few tanks. Fighter squadrons put on an air show overhead. The politicians enjoy the show, and the troops receive good training.

We landed in Cairo Sunday evening, June 9, and breezed

through customs without visas or military orders. We needed only our red official passports. Being military, we were required to use them instead of the blue civilian passports, though I carried mine anyway, for extra measure.

Monday morning, Bob Martin went to the U.S. Embassy to obtain permission for us to visit the Bright Star site.

"I'm afraid they told me it will take a few days to get clearance to visit the site," he said. We were frustrated. We managed to maneuver around the predicament by finding the information we needed for our work from an air force sergeant at the embassy outpost in Giza. He was well acquainted with the site and supplied details about electrical utilities, roadways, and water wells.

Before returning to the hotel, we stopped to photograph the pyramids at Giza. We were swamped by local vendors selling beads, camel rides, and guided tours. For ten dollars, Abdul and Company offered a package deal, which included both the full tour and a camel ride west across the Sahara.

Abdul explained, "A photograph of the great pyramid from the west would be magnificent as the bright sun shines behind you." As we mounted the camels and rode off into the sunset with Nasser, the camel driver, Abdul was waving and smiling. I looked again, and Abdul was gone. What he had not explained was that our ten dollars paid for only a one-way ticket. From half a mile out into the desert, Nasser said, "Your return trip costs twenty more dollars." Keith started to get angry, and Nasser added quickly, "Your return ticket includes an orange soda."

On Tuesday, June 11, we met with U.S. Embassy officials, who I was told were not very dependable. They helped us schedule a trip to Alexandria, on the Mediterranean coast. Our navy officers were to meet with their Egyptian counterparts to review plans for the joint amphibious landing. I needed to look at the port where our ships would unload their supplies and vehicles. I didn't hang around the embassy very long after I learned that a car bomb had exploded outside the building the week before.

Tuesday evening we walked the streets of Cairo. The streets were jammed. They always were, well into the night. We had to step over people sleeping on the sidewalks. Areas beneath the bridges had become small encampments, complete with tents, campfires, and goats.

Returning to our hotel, I switched rooms, moving from the back of the building to the front, overlooking the Nile. The tour books said it was a must view, but they didn't mention the roar of the traffic. It didn't subside until 2:00 A.M. Three hours later, I awoke as the bright desert sun rose over the city. It was an eerie sight, the mosques capped with golden domes and spiraled towers amid old limestone buildings, rising out of a still, gray fog that hung over the river.

Wednesday morning we were to leave at 6:00 for Alexandria. The U.S. Embassy was to send cars, but none showed. By 7:30 A.M. the hotel had found three cars and drivers for us.

Off we went, with no air-conditioning, fifteen of us crammed into three Peugeot station wagons. It was no way to convoy across the desert.

Despite the discomfort, I absorbed another irony of the Middle East. Near the Cairo Zoo, we passed by a woman dressed in black, with two little babies, begging by the roadside. I wanted to stop and give her money, but our Egyptian driver laughed.

"This woman is from a wealthy family," he said. "They own camels, sheep, and goats. She only comes into town to beg to pick up extra money."

The road to Alexandria is a four-lane highway built on sand. It bobs through the desert like a cork on the ocean. Road crews were everywhere, digging up blacktop and shoveling in more sand. I noticed the sand contained a lot of rock, which would be good information for our engineers in planning emplacements for artillery and tanks.

The outskirts of Alexandria are very beautiful, with marshlands and tall reeds, except they dump their garbage among the reeds. The people living in the streets absorb everything useful, and what's left over goes into the marsh. Fishermen stand and fish off the garbage piles.

I made a mental note not to order seafood.

We worked our way through heavy traffic before reaching the Egyptian naval base on the coast of Alexandria.

They weren't ready for our visit. We waited an hour to see the Egyptian admiral. He said we were three weeks ahead of the schedule agreed to earlier by American and Egyptian planners.

"We didn't expect you until One July; our people have not

completed their planning. We'd appreciate it if you'd come back in July," he told us.

I gave our naval commander a withering look; he and others in the group looked disappointed. The Egyptian admiral eventually relented and said as long as we were there, we could try to work out any problems and gather the information we needed.

That in itself presented some difficulties. Although the U.S. and Egypt are on good terms, there's a tension between some of their military people and ours. They don't trust us. This was borne out on Thursday, back in Cairo. We were returning from a meeting with the minister of their water department. The driver, sent by the embassy along with the cars due the day before, obviously was an Egyptian Intelligence officer. We knew that because he kept getting lost. We kept traveling the same streets over and over, passing the same billboard advertising Old Spice four times and snarling up in the same traffic jam at least twice. The driver pretended not to understand English but strained to overhear every word we said.

Finally, we lost our cool and told him to take us back to our hotel immediately. Suddenly, in the outside lane of the Cairo expressway, the car jerked to a halt, and, muttering something in Arabic, the driver got out and opened the hood. The car was a Chevette, and it seemed to be running fine.

As he lifted the hood, I reached over, started the engine, shifted the car into gear, and began to drive away. The driver ran alongside, pounding on the window, but I had the door locked. I refused to allow him back into the car unless he agreed to drive us back to the Nile Hilton. Suddenly, his comprehension of English improved substantially.

He probably had a tape recorder concealed under the dash. I still wonder how his superiors reacted to our long-winded discussions—talking about what we were going to have for dinner and where would be a good place to shop, comparing notes on kids and the like—and what they must have thought of the sounds of the guy pounding on the window and pleading to get back in the car.

The Egyptians are right to keep their guard up, however. I learned during the trip that during the last Arab-Israeli war, the Egyptians lost two live SAM missile sites in a field surrounded by decoys. None of the decoy sites were hit. This showed a need for much better security, particularly when dealing with countries that are also friendly with Israel.

We finished all of our work on Thursday, celebrated with pizza and beer at the Milano Cafe, and shopped at a bazaar in back of the Cairo Hilton. I bought a tiny gold Kartusch medallion for Cheri and had her name engraved on it in Egyptian hieroglyphics. For Meredith, I bought a little French jumpsuit and, for myself, a set of four statuettes of pharaohs and slaves. The shopkeeper insisted they were authentic relics from an ancient tomb. I also purchased an ebony carving of a lion, with ivory eyes and claws.

We had a choice of staying over for a day or catching an early flight home. Keith and Bob decided to stay an extra day and tour the ruins at Memphis.

I was looking forward to experiencing my first Father's Day, so I called Cheri to let her know I would be landing in Chicago on Friday evening, June 14.

But when I called Pan Am to confirm my reservation, I found there was no available flight to Rome, where I had to make a connection to New York. I switched back to TWA, which had a flight from Athens to New York. Departure time from Cairo was to be 6:30 A.M., but we were told to be at the airport four hours early in order to clear customs.

I checked out of the hotel with a navy captain, an air force pilot, and a marine colonel. It was 1:30 A.M. We thought we could catch a nap at the airport. No way. Cairo's airport terminal is an impressive stone and marble structure, but it is also home to hordes of rats, bats, and pigeons. Sleep would have to wait. We holed up at a soda bar, sipping cappuccino as a young boy shined our shoes. He asked us for fifty cents American; we each gave him a buck. After he finished, he clambered up on a stool and had an orange soda with us. He told us that the shoe-shine business had been slow. I told him to check out the camel-ride business.

For two hours, we inched through a long line to the ticket counter, only to be told that TWA's morning flight from Athens to New York had been canceled the day before. We had been rescheduled on a later afternoon flight. The other three military men with me were connecting from New York to either Washington or Atlanta and had no problem with the afternoon flight. But I was destined for Chicago and would miss the last connection.

After about half an hour of flight-shuffling, the ticket agent said, "I've got some good news for you. I've scheduled you on an earlier flight from Rome to New York. You'll have a forty-five-minute stopover in Athens.

"I got you the last seat on TWA Flight 847 from Athens to Rome."

"Great," I said. "That's great news."

The flight from Cairo to Athens took off an hour and fifteen minutes late. Flight time was supposed to be about three hours. With only a forty-five-minute layover, I was sure I would miss Flight 847. I went up to the cockpit—maybe the pilot could fly a little faster.

"Relax. Don't worry about it," the pilot laughed. "This is the same airplane that's going to Rome."

Just before landing, the pilot announced, "It's 9:30 A.M. in Athens; the weather is sunny and eighty degrees. All passengers going on to Rome via Flight 847 will have to deplane and reboard after passing through the gate area. But you won't have to go through customs again."

I checked my tickets and discovered I would have the same seat—4D, on the aisle in the first-class section.

"Can I just leave my carry-on luggage on the plane?" I asked the flight attendant.

"Better not," she said. "We change crews here. No one will be guarding the airplane, and it might not be safe."

We loaded into green shuttle buses for the ride to the terminal. My friends, the navy, air force, and marine officers, gathered at a ticket counter, trying for seats on Flight 847. They too were anxious to get home early, but the plane was sold out. They were stuck with the later flight. I bade them farewell and headed for the security lane to check in.

TWA personnel ran the gate security and had the usual equipment—a wishbone metal detector with flashing red and green lights and a conveyor and screen showing X-rays of the baggage. A young girl, maybe sixteen or seventeen, sat on a high chair, monitoring the screen. She had brown hair and brown eyes and was wearing a plaid skirt. She looked tired and bored.

I placed my briefcase and duffel bag on the conveyor. As I walked through the metal detector, I glanced at the X-ray screen. In the duffel bag, I had one of the small stone statuettes and the ebony lion, some books, and my shaving kit. The shaving kit contained one of those fabled do-everything Swiss Army knives. The knife had shown up in every airport security system I had been through until now. The X-ray screen showed nothing but a large black blob in the center of my bag.

I started to ask the security guard if he wanted to look inside the duffel bag, but he was more interested in my briefcase, which contained nothing but papers. I flashed my official passport, which is supposed to assure some sort of diplomatic immunity against unwarranted searches. But the U.S. and Greece haven't been on the best of terms lately. Two gruff, middle-aged men who I believe were from Greek Intelligence pawed through my papers and ordered me pat-searched.

Something isn't right here, my instinct told me. I could have a fifty-pound bomb in that duffel bag, but these characters only want to rifle my briefcase.

It didn't make me feel any better when a man in a white suit shoved into the passenger line and stuffed a satchel between bags on the X-ray conveyor.

The metal detectors went off when the man passed through the arch. His arms shot straight up, as if he were ready to surrender. The security guard grinned, had him remove his keys and rings and pass through the gate again, then waved him on through.

In a few minutes, we boarded buses and rolled out to the runway. The Boeing 727 carries 145 passengers and a crew of 8. Most of the passengers were Americans, including a large group of Holy Land tourists with two Catholic priests. I noticed a couple of children in the group.

Many of the passengers had the look of typical tourists. One family boarded the plane carrying backpacks and wearing hiking shorts, knee socks, and running shoes. Several older European women were traveling in pairs. There also were some American businessmen carrying briefcases.

I was worried about my luggage, so I asked the flight purser if she could check to see that it had made it onto the right plane.

The purser was a striking woman who appeared to be in her

mid-thirties. About five-foot-nine, she stood ramrod straight, as if she were a soldier. Her eyes were clear blue and soft. Her blonde hair was set in waves and curled up at her collar. She spoke flawless English with a slight German accent. Her name was Uli Derickson.

I explained that my two suitcases had two flight tags, one for Flight 847 and the other for the later afternoon flight. I was concerned, I told Uli, because my bags contained U.S. government papers.

"Sorry," she said, "but there is no way we can contact the baggage claim area, and we can't check all the baggage in our cargo hold."

I mumbled thanks, with visions of my bags headed for who-knows-where dancing in my head. So much for first-class service at three times the price, I thought.

From that point on, Uli was aware that I had official connections to Uncle Sam. I wasn't in uniform; we don't travel in military dress overseas. My official passport was in my jacket, which another flight attendant hung in a closet across the aisle.

I took a magazine from my briefcase, spun the combination lock, and stowed it in the overhead compartment. The briefcase contained my military health records, which identify me by name, rank, and unit; my blue civilian passport; and some army notes on Operation Bright Star. I stashed the duffel bag under the seat in front of me.

The cappuccino I'd drunk in Cairo was working on my system, but I had decided to hold off on using the rest room at the Athens airport, which is not noted for having clean johns. Waiting, I would soon discover, was a mistake.

Flight 847 lifted off at 10:00 A.M., an hour and a half late.

I was back in seat 4D, on the aisle and close to the front of the plane. I introduced myself to the man seated to my right. He was a retired army engineer now working in Africa for a big U.S. company. He lit his pipe as I reached for a cigarette. The "fasten seat belt" sign blinked off, and I heard the muffled pounding of footsteps to my rear. As I turned my head and glanced up, two men rushed by, toward the cockpit, which was about fifteen feet ahead of my seat.

Uli, now wearing an apron, stepped out of the galley. One of the two men leaped into the air and dropkicked her in the chest, slamming her against the wall.

The other man began pounding on the cockpit door with a chrome-plated, pearl-handled .45 automatic—cocked. His companion fumbled with the pin of a hand grenade.

They were literally jumping up and down now, screaming something in Arabic, then, in broken English, "Come to die! Americans die!"

Uli was jerked to her feet and, with the muzzle of a .45 to her ear, began talking into the wall phone.

I stared at the hijackers' faces.

They looked terrified.

No, not terrified. Insane.

They looked insane.

They're on a suicide mission, I thought.

2
The Family

Ed Carlson leaned back in his chair, feet up, and flipped through the TV channels to find the Cubs game.

"Aren't you supposed to be leaving for O'Hare to pick up Kurt?" his wife, Vie, called from the kitchen. The clock on the wall read 3:20 P.M. Ed had been minding his son's affairs during his army mission in Cairo and had taken off early that Friday afternoon.

"I don't have to leave until Cheri calls. She's supposed to let me know when Kurt's plane leaves New York. If I leave then, we'll both get there at the same time," Ed said. "His flight must be running late. But I guess that's better than being stuck on that airplane that was hijacked this morning."

"What airplane was hijacked?" Vie demanded, alarmed.

"Some airplane flying out of Athens—it's been on radio and TV. They just had something on Cable News Network saying the plane has landed in Algiers and the hijackers are beating up the passengers. It wasn't Kurt's plane, so don't go getting yourself worked up."

Vie has a large measure of that thing called "mother's instinct,"

15

a psychic sense of knowing—somehow—when one of her kids is in trouble. She had learned over the years to pay attention to those uneasy feelings, and she wasn't about to push them away now.

"How do you know it wasn't his plane?" she asked.

"Athens—a TWA flight out of Athens, Greece," said Ed.

"Maybe he was flying out of Athens," Vie said.

"Will you forget it?" Ed snapped.

The head of the Carlson clan is not one to jump to conclusions, but he also learned over the years to pay attention when Vie gets a feeling that something is wrong. Quietly, he slipped to a bedroom telephone and called Cheri at the office.

"I haven't heard from Kurt, Cheri, have you?"

"Well, no, Dad, but I suppose his flight is delayed. Honestly, the way Kurt described all the connections he had to make, it'll be a miracle if he's here by morning," she laughed.

"By the way, you know a plane was hijacked out of Athens, a TWA flight," Ed said.

"Well, Kurt's on TWA, but there are a lot of flights," Cheri replied, unworried. "The odds against his being hijacked are a thousand to one," she added, still happily anticipating his return sometime that night.

"I think you'd better check with TWA," Ed said coolly.

She had no more than hung up the phone when it rang again. It was Vie, calling from the kitchen phone where Ed couldn't overhear.

"Cheri," she asked, "by any chance was Kurt flying TWA?"

"I don't know. I haven't heard from him yet," Cheri said calmly.

Vie Carlson's maternal instinct shifted toward high anxiety.

"Cheri, hang up this phone and get ahold of Gini right now." Gini Gaylord, Kurt's travel agent, had booked his flights to Cairo and home.

"OK. If it will make you feel better, I'll check."

At 5:00, the travel agent called back. "Good news, Cheri. Kurt was booked on that flight—uh, 847, it was. But the plane was overbooked, and he was bumped to a later flight. He'll get to New York late tonight, and the airline will put him up at a hotel. He'll be able to get a good night's rest, and you'll see him in the morning."

Whew! Cheri literally ran out of her office and yelled, "Wow, what a close call Kurt had!" The office staff dropped their work to listen.

"Kurt's a lucky Scorpio, that's what he is! That Kurt has always been lucky. He just missed getting on that hijacked plane!"

"I'll bet he'll be bragging about that luck," said Martha, the office manager. They all had a little laugh and went back to work.

Cheri phoned Ed with the good news, and the Carlson family breathed a bit easier.

She left the office and went to the grocery store and to dinner with a friend. She returned home at about 9:00 P.M., fed Meredith, and turned on the television set.

"Kurt ought to be calling from New York anytime," she thought. The phone rang a couple of times, and she cut the conversations short expecting Kurt to call soon.

Meanwhile, Vie kept puttering about, trying to stifle her fears. Absorbed in the Cubs game, Ed feigned unconcern, but he too was feeling uneasy.

The Carlsons are a family of contrasts. His wife calls Ed "the big rock" because he always keeps his emotions hidden while assuring everyone else that any crisis will work out, given time. He's a strict father and a successful businessman. His wife Vie, the devoted mother, somehow managed to juggle the rearing of six children with social causes and interests in art and music.

As the eldest son, Kurt was second in command and always took responsibility for his brothers and sisters, even now when all were adults.

Jan, married to an electrician, had been devoting herself to raising their four children and playing viola in the orchestra at her church. Jan was quiet as a child, but came to life as a student at Colorado State. She demonstrated against the war in Vietnam at the same time Kurt was serving overseas.

Brad, five years Kurt's junior, was the family renegade. In 1973, he was twenty-three and still living at home and playing drums with a local rock band when Ed told him it was time to strike out on his own. The family knew Brad was good on the drums, but had no idea that within a few years he would become "Bun E. Carlos," drummer for Cheap Trick, an internationally known rock band. His gold and platinum albums line whole walls in the family home.

Mark is an orthopedic surgeon in Brooklyn, New York. Like Vie, he has two speeds—fast and stop—and it usually takes a wall to stop him. As a kid, he broke his arm four times and was called "Spark" because of his knack for starting sibling spats.

Gini Dee has one child and works in the office of her husband, who is an optometrist. She also is a vocal soloist in church and for social functions. A cheerleader and actress in high school, she was always very outgoing, and gladly assumed responsibility for younger brother Edwin when the four older children left home.

Edwin, now twenty-seven, works with Kurt in the roofing business. They are especially close, being the oldest and the youngest. In fact, it was always assumed that some day Edwin would join Kurt as a partner in the company.

Ed and Vie raised their children with a lot of love and, above all, taught them to love one another. The children remained close to each other after growing up and often turned to each other in times of crisis.

Vie recognizes her tendency to be overly dramatic at times, but this was different. Kurt was in trouble—bad trouble. She just knew it.

She tried to force her fear from her mind. It was nearing 7:00 P.M., and she had a wedding rehearsal in which she was to be the organist. When she arrived, she blurted out, "Oh, boy, am I lucky, did I luck out today! My son was just within inches of being on that hijacked plane. I've got the right God taking care of me." It was as if she were trying to convince herself Kurt was fine, despite her fears.

As soon as she arrived home, she dashed for the phone to call Cheri. There was no answer.

She remembered Cheri had a dinner date with a friend. Ed again tried to reassure his wife.

"Since we haven't heard anything, I figure he has to be on that later flight. He probably won't call until morning," he said.

But Vie wasn't convinced. She called the travel agent. Gini had kept trying to check Kurt's flights, but TWA had suddenly clammed up. The travel agent was becoming alarmed, too.

At about 9:30 P.M., Vie walked over to Kurt and Cheri's house.

"Cheri," she said, "there's a chance Kurt is on that hijacked plane. Gini is checking on a late flight into New York. She says if

Kurt's name isn't on the passenger list, we'll know he is on the one that was hijacked."

"Oh, no," Cheri said, on the verge of tears.

Vie returned home to wait. Cheri tuned in the 10:00 P.M. news coverage of the hijacking. The TV news services were playing recordings of radio transmissions in which the pilot of the airplane was pleading with the Beirut airport for permission to land.

"They are threatening to kill the passengers. . . . We must get fuel. . . . They are beating the passengers! They are beating the passengers! They are threatening to kill them now! They are threatening to kill them now!"

The unmistakable sounds of someone being beaten could be heard in the background.

The telephone rang, and Cheri ran for it. That's Kurt, surely, that's Kurt, she told herself.

It wasn't Kurt. It was General Baratz, Kurt's commander in the army reserves.

"Cheri, there may be a possibility that Kurt is on that plane hijacked today. I don't want you to get too upset, but I wanted you to know we are checking to find out for sure."

Cheri screamed. "Kurt's on that plane, isn't he? You already know it; that's why you called."

"Please, Cheri, we're not sure. I said there's a possibility. Try not to worry too much."

Cheri hung up, on the verge of hysteria.

She immediately called Vie, and within minutes Ed and Vie arrived from their nearby home. They held each other tightly, both women in tears. Even stoical Ed had begun to cry.

Mark Carlson seldom watches television, but he was tired this Friday evening and plunked himself down in front of the television set. He flipped the dial in search of a ball game, just as his dad had done earlier that day, a thousand miles away—except Mark was looking for a Mets game. Unable to find his beloved Mets, he settled for a news special on the TWA hijacking. After a while he fell asleep.

The telephone woke him, and Mark pushed himself out of the sofa and loped into the kitchen to answer it. His eyes locked onto the microwave oven's clock: 12:32 A.M..

"Mark," his mother's voice said, "don't get upset, but—"

Mark tensed. Whenever Vie says, "Don't get upset," bad news follows.

Kris, his wife, came into the kitchen at that instant and saw the look on Mark's face. "Did somebody die?" she asked.

Vie continued, "I think your brother is one of those on the airplane that was hijacked."

"I've been watching that on the news," Mark said.

"Can you call TWA to see if Kurt was on a later flight to New York?" Vie asked.

Mark hung up, then dialed TWA. He let the phone ring about forty times. No one answered. He found a different listing in Manhattan. A woman answered. "We are not allowed to give out the passenger list," she coolly responded to Mark's urgent questioning. "I think my brother was on the hijacked flight, and I'm trying to find out," Mark persisted. The TWA clerk apologized for not having any information, but took Mark's name and phone number, promising someone would call. It was the first of many unkept promises to call back.

What to do next? It's the middle of the night, Mark thought. He tried Kennedy Airport.

"Where would late passengers who missed connecting flights be put up by TWA?" he asked the information desk.

"They generally use the Viscount Hotel," the desk replied.

Mark called the Viscount.

"Well, as a matter of fact, I have that passenger list right in front of me," the hotel clerk told Mark. She checked for Kurt Carlson. He wasn't on the list.

Mark now expected the worst. The television reports were now saying someone had been killed on the hijacked plane. They thought it was someone from the marines.

He looked at the clock—1:57 A.M. His phone rang. It was Vie.

"Now Mark, don't get upset. I'm sure we have nothing to worry about, but . . ."

Mark interrupted, "I know. We have the TV on, too."

He hung up, a sick feeling coming over him.

What if Kurt were traveling in his uniform? God, he loves to wear that uniform. It would be just like him to have it on. So that's it, he's the one who's been killed, Mark thought to himself.

Back to the phones. Lebanese consulate in New York. No answer. U.S. State Department. "Hello, this is Mark Carlson, and I think my brother is on that hijacked plane. Please help me get some information on what is happening to him," Mark pleaded.

"I'm sorry, sir, we have no information on that," the mechanical voice on the other end said.

"Well, can you tell me who else to call? We have to know."

No, they didn't know who else to call. "Give me your phone number, and someone will return the call." He gave the number, suspecting correctly that nobody would call back.

It was nearing 4:00 A.M. Mark was desperate. Aha! What about the television networks? He was getting more information from the news broadcasts than from official sources, so why not see if they could help? He called CBS.

"My name is Mark Carlson, and I think my brother Kurt is on that hijacked plane. I'm worried sick because you're reporting a marine has been killed, and I think it might have been Kurt, because he was in the Middle East on military business for the army reserves."

"We have the passenger list here. Yes, there is a K. Carlson listed. So it appears he is on it. Our latest report says the one killed was a black man with a crew cut," a reporter told him.

"Kurt's white," Mark said with relief in his voice.

He gave the reporter his name and telephone number and agreed to give an interview the following day, then hung up. The phone rang instantly. It was Vie.

"Mark, TV says the man killed was black, so it can't be Kurt," she said.

"I know, Mother. I just talked to CBS about it. They have the list of passengers. His name's on it. They're going to have Dan Rather's executive secretary call me back later. They want to talk to me some more."

"Well, I sure hope you didn't tell them Kurt is in the military."

"Uh, of course not, Mother, of course not."

Mark could have kicked himself. "Gotta go, Mom," he said and abruptly hung up. He frantically dialed CBS again and asked for the newsroom.

"Listen, I just told my mother I didn't tell you what I told you—you can't say anything about Kurt's being in the service. It could endanger my brother. Please don't use that information."

"We'll keep that out of the news. We are not interested in endangering American lives," the reporter said.

Mark, exhausted, grabbed some sleep, at least secure in his knowledge that the media wouldn't go babbling on about Kurt's being in the army.

CBS had said they would keep Mark and Kris abreast of the latest developments. Throughout the ordeal to follow, the State Department provided absolutely no information to Mark, who became disgusted with them. CBS, on the other hand, phoned constantly, anytime there were new reports about the hostages in general and especially about Kurt.

It was 3:00 P.M. Saturday, the second day, before the news caught up with Bun E. Carlos. He was in Buffalo, New York, waiting to work his magic on the stage of Memorial Auditorium.

The "Carlos" moniker had been concocted several years ago, as a kind of satirical comment on stage names and rock and roll hype in general.

"Carlos," of course, couldn't come from anyplace as ordinary as the Midwest. No, Señor Bun E. Carlos hailed from down Venezuela way, a local rock and roll legend. Didn't he meet with Che Guevara in the mountains back in '61?

Rolling Stone "exposed" the Carlos myth in a cover story on Cheap Trick in the early eighties. But the name stuck, and to this day the whole family calls him Bun.

He'd been on the road eleven days with Cheap Trick, which was opening for REO Speedwagon. Cheap Trick's members and REO had been friends for years, because REO hailed from Champaign, Illinois, and both groups had been on the dreary Illinois bar circuit for years of dues-paying. Bun was up for this tour, because Cheap Trick's long-awaited album, *Standing at the Edge*, was due for release. It had been more than two years since their last album.

Now, Bun wandered aimlessly through the corridors of the Memorial Auditorium in Buffalo, only half-hearing the microphone checks by the sound crew. It was five hours to show time, and there was little to do.

Bun heard the PA system page Paul Korzelius, Cheap Trick's road manager. He knew it had to be an important phone call to merit a holler over the PA system. A few minutes later, Korzelius, an anxious look on his face, hurried down the corridor.

"Hey, Bun," he said, "you hear the news about that hijacking?"

"What hijacking?" Bun replied. He wasn't in the habit of reading newspapers or watching television on the road.

Korzelius gave him a condensed Dan Rather. "Some crazy terrorists hijacked a plane out of Athens and took it to Algiers or Beirut, or wherever, and nobody knows what's happening to the people on board, and your brother is on it."

"My brother is what?"

"Your brother is on the hijacked airplane. He's a hostage."

"Just like that, you tell me my brother is being held hostage by some wacky towelheads? Jesus God, I gotta call home."

"No, no, that isn't necessary," Korzelius said. He explained that Ken Adamany, Cheap Trick's manager, had been in contact with the family in Rockford.

"They say for you not to worry. They'll keep on top of things and let you know what's happening. Your parents don't want anybody to know. It has something to do with your brother being in the army reserves. They're afraid if word gets out he could be in serious trouble, so they want you to keep going as if nothing is happening."

Bun headed for the bus and sprawled on a bunk with his arm over his eyes. He had played the USS *Eisenhower* off Beirut on a USO tour a couple of years back, and he remembered from conversations with servicemen aboard how volatile the Middle East situation can be.

This isn't good, he thought. Kurt isn't the type to sit still and let a bunch of fanatics push him around. He could get himself killed.

His mind flashed back to his childhood days—his first days in school, when his older brother, in the sixth grade, already had that military bearing and the sense that right is right is right and that's it. Kurt had always walked him to school—his protector, never afraid.

He tried to remember the last time they had talked, couldn't, and felt pangs of guilt. With his concert tours and Kurt's involvement in business and the army reserves, they could never seem to get together for more than a quick hello and see-ya-sometime.

God, if something happens to him, I end up the oldest son in the family, and I can't handle that, Bun thought, feeling even guiltier for thinking such a thing.

"This isn't getting me anywhere," he said aloud. "I gotta get my mind together and deal with this. Kurt isn't stupid. He's got himself a kid after wanting one all those years, and he isn't going to risk leaving her without a father. He'll play it cool. He's tough. He can take anything those yahoos dish out. But he's going to need help."

Pushing himself from the bunk, he found a telephone and dialed a number. Briefly, he explained about the hijacking.

"That Lebanese gunrunner we met in Germany—find him," Bun said.

"We may be able to do even better," the voice on the other end said.

Bun found Korzelius waiting, worried, in the corridor.

"We go on with the show," Bun said. "But don't tell anybody my brother is on that plane, except for the other guys in the band. They need to know why I'm acting weird."

3
The 847 Position

Thousands of thoughts flashed through my mind during those first terrifying seconds. The most chilling was of the Kuwaiti airliner that had been blown up just a week before after being hijacked to Iran. Two Americans had been killed. This plane was full of Americans.

Iran, I thought. They're taking us to Iran.

With olive complexion, razor-cut black curly hair, and dark eyes with heavy, black eyebrows, the two hijackers had to be either Palestinians or Iranians.

They wore identical white leisure suits, black linen shirts with flared collars, and black leather shoes with wide soles.

Both had slender builds, partially disguised by their wide pants and padded shoulders.

The short one was about five-foot-six and I guessed maybe twenty-four years old. He had a round face with a distinctive black moustache and a fanatical look in his eyes. He kept shouting and screaming in Arabic and yelling at Uli Derickson in German.

Another Hitler, I thought.

The taller one, about five-foot-nine, I guessed to be about twenty years old. His face was long and rectangular, with a high forehead and close-set eyes. He had the uncanny ability to move each of his eyeballs separately. They darted around like Ping-Pong balls. He had the look of a real live bogeyman, more than just insane. He's crazy, I thought, absolutely crazy.

He stood to the right of Uli, the chrome-plated .45 in one hand and a bag of grenades slung from his shoulder. With his free hand, he continued pounding on the locked cockpit door as Uli, head down, talked on the phone to the pilot. To Uli's left, Hitler held a gray fragmentation grenade close to his own face, fumbling frantically with the safety pin. He was holding the grenade backward!

I knew the pin wouldn't come out the way he was trying to pull it, and for an instant I thought this would be the time to overpower them.

Quickly, I unsnapped my seat belt, half stood up, and looked around. No one else seemed to be reacting. I can't take them alone, I thought, easing back into my seat. A blast from either a grenade or that .45 could be enough to send the airplane into a tailspin that would kill us all.

Keeping my eyes on the hijackers, I took my wallet from my back pocket, glanced down, and slipped out my military ID card. I knew instinctively that being in Uncle Sam's military service could put me in extra danger. If they discovered I was an officer, I would be dead.

Peeling off the plastic laminate and eating the paper was the old military solution, but I worried that they might find the plastic and become more suspicious.

Moving cautiously so as not to catch their attention, I pushed the ID card between the cushions and up the back of the seat. I felt a cloth loop below, which I hoped would catch the card if it started to slide back down.

I worried about that card falling out for many of the long and terrible hours that were to follow.

By the time I had the card hidden, Hitler had managed to pull the pin from his grenade and was holding it up, shaking it and screaming threats that needed no translation.

The plane's intercom clicked on, and Uli lifted her head. Her face looked stressed, and there were tears in her eyes. Crazy placed the .45 alongside her head. Hitler squeezed her shoulder with his left hand and held the live grenade close to her face.

Uli took a deep breath and, speaking as calmly as she could, announced to the passengers:

"The plane is being hijacked. I've spoken with our pilot, and he has agreed to cooperate with the hijackers and take them wherever they wish to go. For the sake of everyone's safety, we must do exactly as we are told."

Hitler gave Uli more instructions, in German.

If they don't speak English, my mind said, there must be a third hijacker somewhere back in the plane. It would be idiotic to take over a planeload of Americans without speaking the language.

But then, a lot of what was happening didn't make sense—like a leisure-suited terrorist who was slow to pull a grenade pin.

Repeating Hitler's orders, Uli told the passengers in first class to move to the rear of the plane. There were twelve of us. We walked down the aisle, everyone tense and scared. I could see terror in the faces of the other passengers, too. I heard someone whimpering, several mumbled prayers.

I searched faces, back and forth, trying to spot the third hijacker. I singled out a young man seated near the front of the coach section. He had dark skin and black hair, and, more importantly, his face betrayed no emotion.

Midway down the aisle I saw an empty window seat on the right. An older, distinguished-looking woman was in the outside seat, and a young woman was holding a baby girl in the center seat. The baby was quiet, but the young mother looked terrified. I thought of Cheri and Meredith.

I took a quick glance over my shoulder. Crazy was jumping up and down, still pounding on the cockpit door. Hitler was yelling something at Uli.

I ducked down, slipped past the two women, and slid into the window seat. Here, in the middle of the coach section, I reasoned, I'd blend in better with the other passengers and have a better vantage point—and possibly help the young woman with her baby.

With Hitler close at her heels, Uli came down the aisle, repeating over and over, "Please, no talking, no talking for any reason.

Everyone put your heads down and clasp your hands over your head."

That was our introduction to what I came to call the "847 position," a physical and mental torture that would test all of us beyond the point of endurance. We were to remain in this frozen pose for most of the next six hours.

The other first-class passengers were placed in rows near the back of the airplane. Then, one at a time, men were shifted at gunpoint to the window seats, where, the hijackers knew, they'd be less of a threat than on the aisle.

Armrests were folded to make room as four people were forced into each row of three seats.

With a viciousness bordering on hysteria, the hijackers forced everyone to be absolutely silent.

If anyone moved or uttered a sound, Hitler pounced, karate-chopping people across the backs of their necks, striking some with the barrel of a .45. With a screaming leap three feet into the air, he kicked one elderly woman in the face, shattering her glasses.

I wanted to stand up and smash his face but forced myself to keep down and avoid attracting attention. My legs, shoulders, and back already were beginning to ache from the cramped, bent-forward position. I could feel my laced fingers and hands growing numb from loss of circulation.

Now Hitler was pushing Uli down the aisle, collecting passports. As she reached my row, Hitler was one row behind, studying people's faces.

I kept my eyes on Hitler. "My official passport is in the closet, and my regular passport is in my briefcase with military papers," I whispered.

"Don't worry about it," Uli said, moving on as if she had collected my passport. Obviously she had remembered our conversation when I boarded the plane and knew that I had official government ties that could put me in danger. For the moment, at least, I was safe.

A few minutes later, with all the passports in a bag, Hitler came around, trying to match faces to the passport pictures.

Snapping off my glasses, I stuffed them into the seat pocket—

passport photos are legendary for looking like someone other than yourself, and I figured that I might look more like someone else without my specs.

Shuffling through the stack of passports as Hitler studied my face, Uli flashed a picture resembling me before his eyes, then moved to the next row.

Although cramped over in the 847 position, I could hear Hitler behind me, sharply questioning some young men who carried green military ID cards.

I could hear Uli trying to make Hitler understand the word *navy*. He kept shouting, "Marines! Marines!" and "New Jersey! New Jersey!"

The battleship USS *New Jersey* had shelled Beirut, and his hatred was unmistakable.

"No, no, we are not combat troops; we are only construction divers," the navy men said. But Hitler kept shouting, "Marine!"

There was nothing I could do except offer a nervous prayer. I knew the navy divers were in serious trouble, but I worried, too, that my time was coming—and fast.

I know Uli tried to protect me as long as she could, and I couldn't help marveling at her efforts to keep the hijackers under control. She kept moving, talking fast, already beginning to manipulate the hijackers in ways that, no doubt, would save a lot of lives.

Shortly after they returned to the front of the plane, Uli spoke over the intercom. "Listen carefully. Is anyone here a U.S. government diplomat? They have found some official passports, and they have demanded that you identify yourselves immediately! Raise your hand or stand up now, because they will find you."

I heard one of the divers call out that he had an official passport. They went back to talk with him, and as they slowly walked back toward the front of the plane, I decided my chances might be better if I came out into the open.

I stood up and raised my hand.

"FBI! CIA!" Hitler shouted, leveling the .45 into my eyes. The muzzle looked huge.

I shook my head. "Tell him I'm in the army reserves and am only on a one-week tour as an engineer. At home I am a roofing contractor. I do this part-time," I told Uli.

"The less you say, the better—I'll handle it," she said.

She gave it her best shot, talking to Hitler in a firm, soft voice. I don't speak German, but she sounded convincing. She used her hands, trying to make Hitler understand my work. He eyed me suspiciously but walked away. At least Uli had convinced him that, whatever I was, I was not with the FBI or CIA.

Looking beyond Uli and Hitler, I could see that the cockpit door was now open. Flight engineer Ben Zimmermann was studying a map, with Crazy looking on. Zimmermann would suffer much during the hours to follow. He became the hijackers' "whipping boy" in their attempts to force the pilot and copilot to obey their orders. Crazy pistol-whipped Zimmermann, and Hitler beat him with an armrest he had ripped from his chair. One end of the armrest was padded, the other jagged steel.

I was back in the 847 position now, trying to visualize what our situation would be in Iran. Then Captain John Testrake, the pilot, came on the intercom and announced calmly that we would be flying to Beirut, Lebanon.

I thought of the more than 200 U.S. marines who had been murdered in their bunker by a suicide bomber and the embassies that had been bombed. We could be in as much danger there as in Iran. I remembered the Jordanian airliner that had been burned at the Beirut airport just two days earlier. But, at least, its passengers had been set free. I felt a strange sense of relief. The hijackers must have some sort of plan beyond pure, wild fanaticism.

I didn't have a deep knowledge of the Middle East. But my mind flashed back to Sunday school lessons and sermons that focused on the never-ending turmoil there as a sign of the fulfillment of frightening Bible prophecies.

We had a two-hour flight ahead of us. I forced the ache in my muscles from my mind, concentrating on finding a way out of this. I had to be ready to help in case a chance to overpower the hijackers offered itself.

One hijacker always remained in the cockpit while the other walked briskly from the front to the rear of the plane, then back again. I timed his patrols—one every five to ten minutes; eight seconds from my seat to the rear and another four seconds back.

Though young and nervous, these men were trained—they were

professionals—despite their bumbling, hysterical takeover of the plane. But something is amiss, I thought. Again it occurred to me that a third hijacker who spoke English had to be hiding, for some reason, among the passengers.

We would have to know who he was before we could try to take them.

The pilot was in command and responsible for all our lives. He and the crew most likely will watch for the right moment and attack, I thought. If they take the one in the cockpit, we'll have to go for the one in the coach section.

If he drops a live grenade, we'll have no more than five seconds to knock him cold and wrap his body around it to try to subdue the blast—and seek out the third hijacker.

I concentrated on forcing my ears open, trying to pick up any sound, perhaps messages being whispered among the passengers. I closed my eyes, slowly turning my head from side to side, straining for any sound. Nothing. Not even from the child in the young woman's lap beside me. She was sound asleep.

The temperature in the airplane was rising, and I figured all the passengers were giving off extra body heat from the pressure. I could feel the sweat on my scalp and my hair curling.

My mind drifted to Cheri and Meredith, and I wondered how long it would be before my family learned of my situation. I daydreamed of being free and calling them to say I was safe and on my way home.

I cut the daydream short and began to figure the odds of my getting out of this alive. I probably had a 50 percent chance of getting murdered, and a 60 percent chance of being killed accidently. That added up to 110 percent—not good odds.

I forced myself to stop thinking about the family and concentrate on surviving. I still needed to learn more about the situation and be prepared physically and mentally for anything, at anytime. Given my rushed departure from Cairo, I hadn't slept for thirty hours, but I willed my body to stay awake and remain alert.

I exercised my muscles with isometrics, flexing different muscle groups for eight to ten seconds. When I pressed my fingers forward and together, the pressure brought blood and some feeling back into my hands. In my mind, I pictured the interior of the airplane and weighed the chances of attacking the hijackers.

I could down Hitler with a sharp blow to the neck as he walked past me in the aisle. With his gun, I could scramble over the seats along the side of the airplane, out of Crazy's line of sight, until I could get in position to ambush him. I was beginning to believe now that there was no third hijacker. It still made no sense, but it seemed rational that, if he was aboard, he would have revealed himself by now. One big problem remained: what to do about those live grenades.

I sneaked a look at my watch. It was 11:45 A.M.—two hours since takeoff. No one had been allowed to use the rest room; everyone remained in the 847 position. I wasn't feeling comfortable at all.

Feeling the airplane beginning a descent, I managed a quick glance out the porthole window to my left. We were definitely coming down. I could see mountains, yellow-colored and barren. No place here for an emergency landing, I thought.

The intercom switched on, and, in almost a routine voice, Testrake announced, "We are making our approach to the Beirut airport."

Suddenly, the 727 turned and climbed over the mountains, and the intercom crackled on again.

"I've been talking with the tower, and they inform me that Beirut airport is closed. We do not have enough fuel to fly elsewhere, so I have told the controller that we will be landing with or without their permission," Testrake said calmly.

We dropped rapidly, banking into our final approach. The maneuver reminded me of an air force landing. It was apparent to me that Captain Testrake was bringing us in as quickly as possible.

"The runway is in view and is being blocked with barricades. After landing, you will probably hear crashing sounds toward the front of the plane, as we break through the barricades," Testrake said.

On the ground, a war was going on. Muslim Druse militiamen were trying to barricade the runway and were under fire from the rival Muslim Amal militia. The Amal won and had barely cleared the runway when we came down, fast and hard.

We bounced, and I thought all the tires would blow out. I looked out the window and saw the wooden barricades scattered alongside the runway. The Mediterranean Sea was parallel with our path. Before we entered the taxiway, Uli and Hitler moved briskly down the aisle, ordering the window shades closed. We came to a halt.

For half an hour, there was not one sound. Outside, we could see through the small cracks at the bottom of our window shades that the sun was shining brightly. Inside, the air had become hot and stale. It smelled too, as not everyone had been able to repress nature's call.

Suddenly, Uli and Hitler strode from the cockpit area and ordered the young mother and her baby to get up. Uli told me the hijackers were allowing some of the women and children to leave the plane. As she led them to the front passenger door, Hitler motioned to me with the .45 to step out into the aisle, turn, and move toward the rear of the plane. I felt the cold steel of his gun barrel against the back of my head.

About two rows in front of me, to my left, was Crazy. He was pulling one of the young navy men from the center seat. It was Bob Stethem.

I looked at Stethem as I was hustled past him. He was stretched back and down, almost flat in his seat. His knees were pushed up, his hands held close at his sides. As they marched me by, I looked hard at his face. I was hoping he'd look at me. I wanted to show him support and encouragement, but he just stared straight down. I'll never forget that look on his face—pure fury, rage, way beyond anger.

They stopped me at row 22. Three older women were told to lift up the armrests and slide together into the two outer seats. Before ordering me into the window seat, Hitler had me remove my tie. He took it in his free hand and stepped out to follow Crazy, who by now was pushing Bob Stethem up the aisle.

Bob was about six feet tall, well built. I don't know how he was chosen by the hijackers. Maybe he was just closer to the front of the plane than the other navy men, but not by much. Whatever the reason, I felt they were putting him off the plane. The military men aboard posed their greatest threat. Then, I had a sick feeling inside. Maybe they're going to start killing us one by one, unless a crazy set of demands is met.

We were on the ground in Beirut for an hour and a half. It seemed like days. The heat was almost unbearable. They still wouldn't let anyone use the rest room.

The passengers were quiet except for an occasional cough; I heard no crying or complaining, even from the children.

I stole a glance up and noticed some of the older men were sitting partway up. The curtain was closed, blocking any view into the first-class section. The hijacker came by my seat and stopped until I was down tight.

Finally, at about 1:30 P.M., the plane took off. There were no announcements over the intercom; we had no idea where we were headed now. I feared the worst: we're going to Iran.

I had another fear, too. The Boeing 727 seemed to be traveling the entire runway before lifting off—a sensation I didn't like at all. Later, Testrake told me he had taken on extra fuel—15,000 to 20,000 pounds over maximum load—to have enough to reach Algiers. The 727 also was overdue for a major maintenance overhaul in Rome.

About half an hour into the air, Uli told us we could sit up straight but not talk. Some people started talking anyway.

"You are threatening all of our lives," Uli warned. She had to get quite adamant with some of the people.

Then she said she would start taking us back to use the rest room. She began leading passengers back one at a time.

Hitler stood guard in the rear of the plane, with Crazy in the cockpit. Hitler made the passengers leave the rest room door open.

When it was finally my turn, Hitler looked away for an instant, and I had to resist the urge to jump him. I could break him in half, take his gun, and go after Crazy—but the grenades still made it too risky. I went back to my seat.

Uli began bringing paper cups of water and hard rolls down the aisle. It was the first water we'd had since the hijacking began. We had been in the 847 position for more than six hours.

I noticed a spatter of blood on Uli's sleeve. That was not a good sign.

I could see now that several people had been taken off the plane in Beirut. I looked out the window and figured we were flying southwest along the coast of Lebanon. I overheard Uli telling one of the navy men that the hijackers wanted to fly to Algeria, but there was some concern that the airport there didn't have equipment to service our plane. She also said something about hiding some wire and razor blades the hijackers had brought aboard.

Hitler paced up and down the aisle with the .45 in one hand and a grenade in the other. He kept replacing and removing the firing pin.

Uli was beginning to look exhausted. I wondered how long she could continue fast-talking Hitler and Crazy. A lot of women and a few children were still on the plane. The children had to be frightened, but none of them were fidgeting.

A woman in the outside seat in my row couldn't seem to sit still or keep her mouth shut. She kept raising her hand and asking to go to the rest room and started whining and complaining. The other two women sitting next to me were getting nervous.

"Lady," I hissed through my teeth, "please shut up. You're going to get us all killed."

She ignored me. Uli came back and warned her to be quiet, but she kept on complaining. I think she was among those the hijackers released early. Hitler and Crazy probably were glad to be rid of her.

An older man sat in front of me, next to the emergency door over the wing. I thought about whispering to him that once the plane landed he could spring the door open. Unless we landed in Iran or Sudan, I reasoned, the 727 surely would be surrounded by a SWAT team. With the first shot, I figured, we could be out the emergency door and home free.

Through the window, I studied the terrain below, trying to figure our destination. But all I could see was water or coastline. From the position of the sun, I could tell we were flying west. That meant we weren't going to Iran.

Once we flew over what looked like a military airfield on the coastline. It seemed to be in the middle of nowhere. I think it was in Libya.

After about four hours, Testrake lowered the nose of the 727, and I knew we were coming in for a landing. As the plane went through a sharp turn and began a fast descent, Hitler ordered us to pull the window shades and get back into the 847 position.

We can't take much more of this, I thought. God, please, bring an end to this soon.

4
Terror at Home

Saturday, June 15, was a blur for the Carlson family. Friends and family had gathered in response to their urgent phone calls, but so far none of Rockford's four television stations, its daily newspaper, or its five radio stations had discovered that a home-town boy was a hostage.

TWA's passenger list said Kurt was from Chicago, home base for his army reserves unit. Once the local media learned that a member of a prominent, fifth-generation Rockford family was aboard Flight 847, all hell would break loose.

But today they were thankful the secret was safe.

In their grief, they didn't want to be hounded by the press and the tons of people who would call as soon as they knew Kurt was on that plane. There's time for all that later, Vie thought.

In New York, Mark and Kris awoke at 8:00 A.M. and immediately resumed their vigil in front of the television set, with radios going in the background. They had barely slept and were on edge.

Vie, Cheri, and Ed, back in Rockford, hadn't been to bed at all. They had spent the night huddled in front of the TV set, which was tuned to Cable News Network. They, too, were bleary-eyed and reaching the point of exhaustion.

By now, Flight 847 had returned to Algiers. The news services were getting more details about passengers being badly beaten and, even more chilling, conflicting reports of people being removed from the plane in the blackness of night at the Beirut airport. Passengers freed in Algiers were saying those who had disappeared were military men or people with "Jewish-sounding names."

"The marine" whose body had been dumped on the tarmac of the Beirut airport still was unidentified. For some reason, the wire services were doubting the report of one freed passenger that the victim was a "black man with a crew cut."

Mark studied his early copy of *The New York Times* in detail, trying to read between the lines. A chill spread through him when he came across a paragraph quoting "United States officials in Cyprus" as saying there were no marines aboard the plane, "although they said there were some navy personnel and an army reservist."

The reservist could only be his brother, Mark knew. His sense of logic told him that, since Kurt would be carrying an official government passport, there was a strong chance he had been singled out by the hijackers and had been beaten, if not killed.

He called his mother in Rockford.

"Have you heard anything more?" he asked.

"No, nothing," Vie answered. Mark noted the exhaustion in her voice. She was subdued and unusually quiet.

"How are all of you holding up?" he asked.

Vie avoided the question. "Bill Giolitto is here helping us," she said.

A friend of Kurt and a fellow Rockford businessman, Giolitto also is a major in the U.S. Army Reserve and the public relations officer for the 416th Engineer Command. He had knocked on the Carlsons' door at dawn, dispatched by his commander in Chicago.

"Bill says it is very important that we continue to keep Kurt's military affiliation out of the newspapers and TV," Vie said. "He says it could put him in danger if the hijackers find out—if they don't know already."

Giolitto would deal with any calls from outsiders and told the

Carlsons they would get their information on the status of the hijacking directly from the military.

Looking back later, the Carlsons see Giolitto's arrival as a godsend—not so much because of his military ties, but because he virtually took charge of a family that was in shock.

Cheri and Vie had both wept throughout the night; no one had slept or eaten. Cheri's eyes were so weary that she had difficulty removing her contact lenses.

Giolitto rustled up some cold cuts and pizza and began making telephone calls up the chain of army command. He wrote down special telephone numbers that were supposed to put the family in contact with military officials with the latest information.

Naturally, the brass let him down. When Ed called the special "hot line," he hung up disgusted. "All they want to do is listen— like a sounding board for gripes. They can't tell us anything. That guy I talked to didn't say two words."

"He probably doesn't know two words," Vie said bitterly.

Giolitto could only shrug helplessly. He knew that Ed and Vie understood army red tape and that no amount of PR snow-jobbing would fly. But at least they seemed to be snapping out of their lethargy somewhat.

"Look," he said, uncomfortably, "I hate to bring this up now, but it's important. The army may want to put taps on your telephone lines—if you don't mind."

"What on earth for?" said Vie.

"Once word gets out that Kurt is on the plane, you'll be getting a lot of calls, and some of them will be from cranks. If we've got taps, we can track them down and put a stop to it."

Vie and Ed didn't exactly like it, but they were too tired to argue.

The television news reports were growing more ominous and contradictory. A marine had been killed. There were no marines aboard the plane. He was a white man with brunette hair. He was a black man with a crew cut. He was in the navy. He was not in the navy.

The passengers who were being freed—mostly women and children—were relating horror stories. Some passengers were being beaten mercilessly, but they were uncertain about who the victims were because they weren't allowed to raise their heads.

In Washington, the White House was talking tough: no way would the U.S. government negotiate with terrorists or give in to their demands.

A special "task force" had been set up in the State Department to figure out what to do. There were "unconfirmed" reports that the Delta Team, an antiterrorist commando squad, was moving toward the Mediterranean.

The hours dragged on. Cheri and Vie became increasingly distraught. Cheri was on the verge of hysteria and at times seemed incoherent. Someone called her doctor and had a prescription for tranquilizers sent over. Late in the night, she gave in to urgings that she go to bed and try to sleep.

Vie couldn't sleep at all. She sat up for hours, reading. She had turned to the only resource she could think of—her Bible.

At about 4:00 A.M. Sunday, she came into Cheri's room and awakened her daughter-in-law.

Together, they talked through their feelings of terror and helplessness, and, in praying for God's help, Cheri, for the first time, asked the Lord to come into her life.

Cheri slept peacefully through the rest of the night. She dreamed of Kurt: Kurt, coming off an airplane, smiling and waving; Kurt, running to her and the baby; Kurt coming home.

She would look back to that dream often during the trials of the next two weeks. To her, it would become like a vision, a promise that her husband would return to them.

Giolitto returned at dawn and was amazed at the change in Vie and Cheri. They were incredibly calm and serene.

"You've heard some good news?" he asked, half afraid the army had goofed up and failed to let him know something important.

"No," Vie said. "It's just that we have decided to put this whole thing in the Lord's hands, where it belongs. If it is His will, Kurt will come out of this all right."

Giolitto went back to the telephone. He seemed to spend a lot of time there, conferring with army brass in far-off places.

The military people seemed concerned about something, Vie noticed.

"Are you sure it's not in the files?" she heard Giolitto saying. "Kurt usually puts that stuff back in the files; he wouldn't take it with him."

Vie assumed he was talking about Kurt's military identification records but decided not to ask. It wouldn't help matters if she found out that Kurt was carrying classified documents that would put him in more jeopardy.

She really didn't feel she could take any more bad news right now, but she got it anyway. At about 11:00 A.M., General Baratz pulled into the driveway with his wife.

Purely social, both the general and Giolitto tried to assure the Carlsons. "We wanted to pay our respects because Kurt is one of our finest officers," the general said.

Vie was not convinced.

"General Baratz, we know from our own checking that Kurt is on that plane. In what condition is he? Was he beaten?"

"Nothing has been confirmed," the general said.

"He's dead, isn't he?" Vie said. "An army general and his wife don't come calling at eleven o'clock on a Sunday morning unless it's bad news."

"He is not dead, Mom," Cheri cut in. "Kurt is a survivor; he is alive. I just know it."

Ed pressed for more information, but the general admitted apologetically that the news services were far ahead of the army in keeping track of the situation. It takes a while for information to funnel down the army chain of command, he explained. "Sometimes we don't get the information until it's one or two days old."

Well, that's the army for you. I see it still hasn't changed, thought Ed, remembering his World War II experiences.

Vie thanked them for coming, and the couple left at noon.

At 1:00 P.M. Mark called from New York. He was on duty at the hospital and had been in surgery all morning, with a radio tuned to the news. Vie, Ed, and Cheri had been listening, too. The latest headlines were not good.

"The man who was killed was not black. The way they are describing him now, it could be Kurt," Vie said quietly.

"I know—heard it, too," Mark said. He hung up the phone, trying to sort his thoughts. He had never been so badly shaken. Kurt is gone, he thought. My brother is dead.

He thought of Kris, at home with the kids. She probably knew. A television crew was waiting for him in the hospital lobby. He would have to compose himself for the interview. He was furious at Reagan and the U.S. State Department; he wanted the world to know. Yet, if there was still a slim chance that Kurt was alive, he must not say anything to worsen his chances. Polite, but critical, that's what he would be.

At home, Kris worried about whether to call Mark with the latest terrifying news. If he's still in surgery, I shouldn't add to his worry, she thought. First, she wanted to find out once and for all if the news reports were accurate. She called CBS.

"We have a picture of the man who has been killed," the reporter said. "I hate to suggest this, but perhaps you could come down and look at it and—well, maybe it isn't your husband's brother."

"Oh, my God," she cried. "It must be Kurt. I just know it."

Her mind raced. Should she try and get Mark out of work for a few hours? She didn't want to see the picture she was sure she would be able to identify. No, it didn't seem fair to make Mark identify his own brother—not fair to his patients, either.

"If it is my brother-in-law, can you drive me home?"

"Of course."

"Can I bring my children down, because I don't have a baby-sitter?"

"Sure."

The boys really didn't understand what was happening to Uncle Kurt. Probably as a defense mechanism, they'd put the incident into their fantasy world. The day before, they'd been playing in their wading pool, and Kris had overheard them. "Sad is Dad, our dad is sad," they'd chant. "The bad guys have Uncle Kurt; let's rescue Uncle Kurt." And they'd jump into the pool. Then they pretended to be "He Man," the television cartoon character, rescuing Uncle Kurt.

No, it would be better to leave them in their fantasyland for a while longer. She hurriedly left them at a neighbor's and drove to Manhattan.

From their home on Staten Island, it took an hour to get to "Black Rock," as the CBS building is nicknamed. Kris decided not to think about the picture, but it came persistently popping back into her head. What am I going to tell Mark? she thought. I'll tell him it doesn't look like Kurt but ask him to come and be sure. It will give me time to prepare him for it.

She entered Black Rock, and was met by a woman who took her

up to the newsroom. She was taken into a tiny viewing room, where four people were standing around. She didn't want to go through with it. I think I'll go home now, she thought.

But it was too late. A man's picture flashed on a viewing screen in front of her. She forced a look.

The man had a pointed nose and hair right down to his forehead. It wasn't Kurt.

"It is not my brother-in-law," she told the people. They hugged her, patted her on the back—they were excited that it wasn't Kurt, too. Then they said, "Here's a phone you can use to call anywhere in the world you want."

She called Cheri's house and reached Ellen, Bun's wife. "It's not Kurt. The dead man is not Kurt!" she yelled into the phone. It was 5:30 P.M., Father's Day.

She didn't call Mark and didn't leave the studio right away, either.

"Would you like to come into the studio and watch Dan Rather?" someone said.

"Well, yes, I would," she responded calmly. Inside she was excited. Here's a story for the family back in Rockford, she thought.

Meanwhile, Mark had arrived home and was worried. Where was Kris? Where were the kids? They were supposed to meet at home around 6:00 P.M.

Mark phoned CBS. "Have you seen my wife?" he asked. "As a matter of fact, she was here, watching Dan Rather. By the way, she identified the dead man as not being your brother."

"Thanks for telling me," he said.

The biggest news of the day, and my wife is watching Dan Rather and forgets to call me, he thought, shaking his head.

5
Prepare to Die

I still had no idea where we were landing, although sometime earlier I'd heard Uli tell one of the navy divers that Hitler wanted to go to Algiers. The airport there didn't have the equipment to handle a 727, she said. All I knew for sure was that we were over a desert moonscape that looked like a scene out of *Star Wars*. Han Solo would feel right at home landing the Millennium Falcon here.

As we banked around steeply, at about a ninety-degree angle, I looked out and saw the airfield. It was a desert strip with a cyclone fence surrounding it.

We came down hard and fast, but at least a bit more smoothly than that first Beirut bounce-down. We ground to a halt without taxiing; just plain stopped at the end of the runway .

It was hot as blazes. You've never experienced sunshine until you've been in the middle of a desert, inside a stuffy airplane full of frightened people with the air-conditioning turned off. The plane began heating up as soon as we stopped. Sweat began pouring from the passengers.

We'd been on the ground for about fifteen minutes when Uli tapped me on the shoulder. Slowly, I raised my head and looked into the barrel of Hitler's shiny .45.

Uli told me to get up, and Hitler marched me up the aisle to the first-class section. I figured I was in for the same thing that they'd done to Stethem, whatever that was. Hitler stopped me at the front row and pushed me down across two first-class seats. He took my wallet and rifled through it, flipping the contents over his shoulder—a few receipts, some Egyptian and American money, traveler's checks, my credit card and driver's license. He seemed angry, as if he hadn't found what he was looking for.

Yanking my arms up behind my back, he tied my hands together with a silk tie, so tightly that it cut into my wrists. Then he blindfolded me with a handkerchief that stank of vomit. It covered my eyes and nose. The smell was nauseating.

Hitler grabbed me by my shirt, pushed me through the cockpit door, and threw me onto the flight deck. I managed to sit up on the steel-ribbed floor, facing the rear of the plane. I pulled my knees up tight to my chin. Nearby, I could hear Testrake and the copilot, Phil Maresca, talking to the control tower.

"Please call the United States Embassy immediately."

The reply came: "Someone is coming from the embassy." I suspected the tower was stalling.

"We need fuel, a full load of fuel," Testrake said firmly.

"You'll just have to wait," they replied. "We have no facilities to refuel you."

Testrake's voice rose in anger. "I called you four hours ago. You knew I was coming, and you told me you'd have facilities here for me to refuel."

"Wait," the tower said.

Strangely enough, although tied up and slumped on the cockpit floor, I felt safe being that close to the crew. Their voices were strong and confident, and they seemed in control of the situation.

The blow came from nowhere, a bolt of lightning, jarring me to the core. Again and again, the weapon—it felt like a nightstick— thudded into my right shoulder blade, then the left, then the right, then the left, five or six times.

"I can't stand this anymore! I have to leave," I heard Uli cry.

My adrenaline began flowing as if I'd been given a giant hypodermic needle of the stuff. My muscles flexed tightly, but I knew I couldn't get loose to give those bastards a fight. Worse yet, I heard not a word of protest from the crew. They just sat there. I couldn't understand it. My confidence in them was shaken, and again I felt alone.

I thought then that the navy diver the hijackers had carried up to the front in Beirut might be near me, lying dead, and that I was next.

Now Testrake was shouting into his microphone.

"They're killing people and beating them. They're beating and killing Americans."

I heard the microphone keyed and realized it was being held close to me. Suddenly, I was being pummeled again—both Crazy and Hitler were kicking me and jumping up and down on my back, one on each side. I had willed myself to be silent when the beatings started but now realized they wanted me to make noise. Screams might convince the tower to refuel us.

I yelled, but I really wasn't feeling any pain anymore. The blows only seemed to interfere with my thoughts. My mind was racing ahead, analyzing my predicament and searching for the slightest chance of fighting back.

I was praying that I would feel no pain; I have always been afraid of pain. I began repeating over and over the lines of the Twenty-third Psalm: "Yea, though I walk through the valley of the shadow of death, I will fear no evil, for Thou art with me; Thy rod and Thy staff, they comfort me."

I felt the heels of the hijackers' leather shoes grinding into the muscles of my back and shoulders, and I gave them more noise, although I could have taken it without a sound. My body felt numb.

The hijackers must have dictated a list of demands through Uli to the pilot, because Testrake now began reading them to the tower.

They wanted Shi'ite prisoners in Israel and Kuwait released. That surprised me, and I thought, This isn't a list of impossible demands, as in a Palestinian-style hijacking. But any demands, no matter how negotiable, would take time—which I might not have.

A fuel deadline was set at fifteen minutes away. I understood now that I was their pawn to get fuel, and I didn't have much time. The body kicks slowed down somewhat as Hitler moved away, leaving Crazy to keep it up.

I could hear Hitler shouting what sounded like religious chants. His voice sounded distant, and I thought he had left the plane, but he was leaning out the cockpit window.

I recognized only one word: "Khomeini!" I could hear a crowd of people outside, chanting and cheering in return. Every time he shouted "Khomeini," the crowd would cheer, and Crazy, as if on cue, would kick me again.

With enemies on the ground and enemies in the plane, we couldn't win either way.

Testrake was still arguing with the tower about fuel. The hijackers set another deadline. It came and went. They set a third deadline.

"What is the status of the fuel?" Testrake called on the radio.

"Wait," the tower replied.

They're stalling, maybe hoping to negotiate with these madmen to set people free, I told myself, and I am caught in the middle. I strained to pick up any sounds from the passengers and crew. None.

Crazy began kicking me again, but I still felt no pain. The wheels in my head were in high gear as I concentrated on what I could possibly do to survive.

I had lost all faith in Testrake. I felt he must be weak: he was just sitting there, cooperating with these lunatics in Beirut and now in Algiers, or wherever we were, while innocent people were being beaten to death. Where would the line be drawn? How many would be killed? Something is terribly wrong here, I thought. I had forgotten that he, too, was a hostage.

I could hear Hitler pacing back and forth, repeating over and over again a terrifying phrase:

"One American must die! One American must die! One American must die!"

I knew then that Bob Stethem was still alive and that I would probably be the one American that "must die."

As the fuel deadline neared, Testrake called the tower again.

"Where is our fuel? We need it now, right now. They're going to begin killing passengers."

The response from the tower was silence.

I could feel the hijacker stepping behind me and turning around; then I heard his body stretch. He took a deep breath, and I flinched, expecting the worst. This could be it.

He let out a piercing scream: "Marine!"

I felt something smashing into the top of my head—once, twice, three times. That final blow was twice as hard as the others.

I saw the American flag, minus the stripes and with a lot more stars. And I prayed, "Lord, keep me conscious so that I can give him noises."

I rocked backward, my head bouncing off the floor, then snapped forward with my face to my knees. He kicked my head back to see if I was still conscious.

I guess I was, because I heard the tower crackling through the radio, "Your fuel is coming."

"Where? I don't see any fuel trucks. When is it coming?" the pilot asked.

The hijacker put the .45 to my head and tried to grab me by the hair, but it's short and he couldn't get a grip, so he twisted his hand into my shirt collar. He dragged me out of the cockpit and dropped me in a heap at the exit door. I heard them set a new deadline for fuel: ten minutes, no more, or "one American must die."

I lay on my side facing the door. The hijacker kicked me in the spine with the toe of his shoe, yelling, "Marine! Marine!"

He pulled me up by my shirt again, and, with the gun barrel pressed against my head, just behind the right earlobe, he held me at the open door and yelled again, "One American must die!"

Abruptly, he dropped me to the floor, closed the door, and stalked toward the cockpit. I resigned myself to the fact that my life would end in ten minutes.

At least I had time to sum it all up and prepare to join my Lord. I had no feeling in my upper body. My throat was parched, and I could hardly breathe.

I asked God to watch over Cheri and Meredith. I prayed for all of my family; they would need special strength to cope with this.

"Help Cheri, Lord, and find someone for her. And take care of little Meredith, for she will grow up without a father," I prayed.

I knew that my father would help, with that stoical strength of his. He would take over my business and run it right. And I had good insurance, so nobody would be hurting financially.

Then I assessed my own life and asked my God to have mercy on me.

I felt a sense of peace. I was ready.

6
Calling Uli

Mark listened intently, trying to make sense of the clamor of the television press conference at the Viscount Hotel in New York. Reporters were shouting questions at Uli Derickson, the flight purser aboard Flight 847.

Already it was becoming clear that Uli's response to the terrorists had gained the release of many of the passengers and may have saved others from being mercilessly beaten or killed.

She had been set free as the terrorists settled in at the Beirut airport, holding Capt. John Testrake and his copilot aboard the plane. The count was still uncertain, but about forty male passengers apparently had been taken off the plane and were somewhere in Beirut. It was now Sunday, June 16.

Mark could see that Uli appeared distraught, perhaps confused by the news hawks.

"What's the condition of the man who was beaten in Algiers?" one of the reporters shouted.

"Poorly, very poorly," Uli replied.

"I've got to talk to that woman, now," Mark told Kris, bolting for the door.

The Viscount Hotel is normally a twenty-minute drive from their home. But the traffic snarled, and it took an hour. The hotel lobby was virtually deserted.

"Where did all the press people go?" he asked the desk clerk.

"Cleared out about five minutes ago."

"The purser, Uli Derickson—what room is she in? I've got to talk to her; my brother is on that airplane, and I have to find out if he is hurt," Mark said.

"Sorry, we were told she is not to be disturbed," the clerk said.

Mark left, frustrated and angry. The television broadcasts of the airplane radio transmissions left little doubt that someone had been viciously beaten, but no one seemed to know how badly. If it was Kurt, and if he could just get someone to describe his injuries, he might be able to use his medical background to assess the damage.

From home, he called the hotel again. No, they would not put through a call. He called TWA. No, they were not allowed to give out telephone numbers of employees. He dialed AT&T information. Of course, they had a listing for Ms. Uli Derickson. He dialed the number.

"She isn't here right now," Uli's husband said after Mark explained that his brother was among the hostages. He promised to give his wife Mark's number, assuring him she would call as soon as she arrived home.

Mark waited. Two hours. A long two hours. He was giving up hope when the phone rang.

Uli sounded calm, professional, reassuring.

"I need to know if you can remember seeing my brother," Mark said. He described Kurt and added, "He was traveling with an official passport. He is in the U.S. Army Reserves, and is a contractor—"

"Yes, yes, of course—he's the one. . . . He was . . . he was . . ."

"What?" Mark said, alarmed. "What happened to him? Is he all right?"

"Please," Uli said, a sob breaking her voice. "I can't talk anymore. Please. Someone will call you. TWA will call you."

"OK, OK," Mark said, anxious not to lose a potentially valuable link to his brother's fate. "Could I call you again, maybe after we know more?"

"Of course," she said. "Call me anytime." She was weeping.

TWA called in less than half an hour.

"Where and how did you get Ms. Derickson's home telephone number?" the caller demanded. "That is not public information."

Mark flared. "I just called information; she's listed in the phone book. Now, what do you know about my brother? Was he the one they were beating?"

"We have no information to confirm that. We will keep you informed," the caller said.

Mark stared at the phone for a long time, a gnawing fear replacing his anger.

"It's bad," he told Kris. "I'm afraid it's very, very bad."

By now, Mark's constant telephone calls had pieced together enough information that gave him an uncannily accurate picture of what had happened aboard Flight 847. He had conned a TWA clerk, for instance, into confirming that Kurt was booked into the first-class section of the airplane.

A woman passenger who had been released told a television interviewer she had seen two people slumped over in the back row of the first-class section, one with his hands tied behind his back and blood trickling from the back of his head. The hijackers were singling out military men. Kurt was a logical choice.

Mark called his mother. He had to prepare her for the worst.

"I suspect that Kurt has been beaten," he said. "Maybe you'd better not tell Cheri yet, but I think you should know in case . . ."

"Do you really think so?"

"I'm pretty sure, but at least it sounds like he's alive. If I can find out more about what kind of injuries he has, I can get a pretty good idea of how bad it is. He could have head injuries."

Vie was quiet on the other end of the line.

"They have to know that he is in the military," Mark went on. "One of the passengers said she heard a man identify himself as army reserve. Maybe that saved his life. But that means he had to be one of the military people taken off the plane in Beirut."

"We will just have to pray and trust in the Lord," Vie said.

"I'm going to wait awhile, then try another call to Uli Derickson," Mark said. "Once she has a chance to calm down, maybe she can tell me more."

A computer answered when Mark tried calling Uli again. The

telephone itself is a wonderful, loving machine that can put you in touch with people you need. But a talking computer has no heart, no love, no compassion.

"The number you have dialed has been disconnected. If you need assistance, please dial your operator."

Beep. Click. Whirrr.

"The number you have dialed has been disconnected. If you need assistance, please dial your operator. The number you have dialed is not in service. . . ."

Click. Buzzzzzzz.

7
The Vision

I had always been the typical Christmas-and-Easter-and-occa-
sionally-with-the-folks churchgoer. Not anymore.

I had been kicked and beaten for one and a half hours. A .45
automatic was cocked at my head. I discovered what God is all
about.

My father and mother are very religious, and I had always gone
to church as a boy, but I had never really joined a church. I was a
Christian, true enough, just not a very devout Christian.

The hijacker kept saying, "One American must die!" He had
given me ten minutes to live.

"Dear Lord," I prayed, "please watch over Cheri and baby
Meredith, now and after I am gone. Please be in their hearts and
give them love, strength, and happiness. Help Cheri always to
remember me, but to find another someday, so that Meredith will
have a father. I love them so much, dear Lord."

Images of Cheri and Meredith flashed through my mind as I
prayed. In one mental picture we were all together, and in another
they were waving good-bye to me. Again and again, I could see
Meredith's face as I sat holding her out by the pool. She looked a
lot like her dad.

I prayed then for myself. "Dear Lord, I've felt you at my side and pray that you will come into my heart. Please forgive my sins and protect me from further suffering. Give me the strength, dear Lord, to fight until I die."

I heard the pilot saying we had five minutes before the fuel deadline.

I closed my eyes and slowed my breathing. My body was numb, almost paralyzed. I felt that I was close to death from my injuries. I asked the Lord to take me so that I would suffer no more.

Then, a vision came into my mind. I could see a figure standing atop a hill of black lava stone. His robes were blue and white, his face shadowed by the brightness surrounding him. His arms, draped in his robes, were extended as if to receive me.

And then I blacked out. I don't know how long I was out. I had lost track of time.

When I came to, my thoughts had changed. "I'm not going to just let them pick me up and shoot me. I'm going to give it one last shot." Never in my life had I given up and quit.

Some feeling had come back into my upper body, and I began trying to loosen the necktie binding my wrists, but the knots only got tighter. Then I started blinking my eyes real hard, maybe hundreds of times, until the blindfold worked down enough so that I could see light over the top of it.

This is my chance, I thought. At least the light would guide me in a desperate plan I had formed. My legs were cramped, but the hijacker hadn't beaten them. I figured that when he picked me up I could kick hard, dive off the plane, hit the ground rolling, and get far enough under the plane so that he couldn't shoot me.

I had been a good wrestler in high school, but there aren't many good wrestling moves you can make with your hands tied. I figured I would come up slowly with my knees and waist bent forward and my head back enough to follow the light. The gun barrel would be just under my right ear. I would slump back slightly, snap my head forward and down, and roll into a tuck until I hit the concrete.

If I was lucky, the shot would graze my head or hit me in the rear. I would still have enough left to crawl under the plane and maybe get up and run like hell.

It was a long shot, but I had decided I'd rather be gunned down running on the ground than be killed in this airplane.

Crazy would probably blow his own head off.

I could hear the crowd outside the airplane, chanting, "Khomeini! Khomeini!" I knew they would probably catch me and drag me back, but at least there was one small chance.

The tower was saying that no one had arrived from the embassy and that the American ambassador could not be reached; he had taken the day off. The tower sounded as if it didn't want to bother with this mess at all.

They were letting more of the passengers off the back of the plane, and that's all that seemed to matter now. Apparently I was expendable.

"We need fuel right now, or they are going to kill a passenger," Testrake told the tower, his voice insistent.

Suddenly, Hitler jerked me up by the collar and jammed the .45 behind my ear.

"One American must die!" he shouted.

I came up on my knees and listened for the door to open. This is it; I'm ready, I thought. The instant I think he is about to pull the trigger, I will dive out that door.

Suddenly, Testrake began shouting, "I see the fuel truck on the runway! The fuel truck is coming!"

The hijacker dropped me to the floor and ran forward. I thought, It was the Lord. I was that close.

"Where is it? I don't see it," said Phil, the copilot.

What a time to question your captain, I thought.

"In your mirror; it just turned up the runway," Testrake said.

"I see it now," Phil said.

Thank God. Things have to get better now, I thought. I was wrong. It got crazier.

"Is it Shell fuel?" the hijacker demanded. "It has to be Shell, or it is no good—not acceptable!"

He insisted on Shell fuel because he considers Shell Arab-owned.

"They say the fuel has to be Shell fuel. I repeat, Shell fuel only, or we go back to square one," Testrake said.

"Look at the sign on the truck," the tower said.

"We can't see it. It must be on the other side. Move the truck around," Testrake said.

Dear God, I thought. My life is on the line, and they are debating the merits of a particular brand of gasoline. Insane!

Luckily, it was a Shell fuel truck.

Then came another long wait—something about a special nozzle to fuel the plane.

Finally, the tower radioed, "We are prepared to fuel your plane but can proceed no further."

"What's the problem?" Testrake asked.

"TWA does not have a charge account here."

Testrake shouted, "You idiots! You jerks! The embassy will pay for the fuel."

After another long wait, the tower responded: "We have no clearance from your embassy to pay for the fuel. They will not authorize payment."

This is too bizarre to be anything but a delaying tactic, I thought—I hoped.

Hitler was getting nervous and started muttering again.

"We have to have fuel, or they are going to kill an American," Testrake said. "They are going to kill an American right now!"

"Does anyone have a Shell credit card?" the tower asked.

The pilot started asking around for a credit card. I was on the verge of volunteering my American Express card when Uli said she had a Shell card in her purse.

They took Uli's card, and I could hear the sound of one of those hand-operated stenciling machines copying the bill.

An airline official told me later that the charge came through on Uli's account in the United States—4,500 gallons of JP-4.

There was some joking about it then, but the hijackers weren't laughing. Nor was I. I was still worried.

The haggling continued for about an hour before the refueling was completed. I heard the pilot say we would be leaving Algiers and flying back to Beirut.

Hitler's raving that "one American must die" kept running through my mind. Even with the fuel, he still might be planning to kill me and dump me off the plane. I had to do something.

So I prayed for the hijackers, asking God to make them merciful toward me. I figured it was probably futile, but there was nothing else I could do.

For a moment, both hijackers were in the cockpit, and Uli walked by me, alone.

I turned my head and looked up over the edge of the blindfold. "Stewardess," I said, "would you please tell the hijacker that I am not a marine? Tell him that I have a family—a wife and a baby girl back home."

Uli stared at me for a moment, surprised that I was still alive. Hitler returned, and she placed a hand on his shoulder and translated what I had said into German.

I could feel the airplane beginning to taxi as Hitler looked down at me. Then he stepped in front of Uli and lifted me up, standing me in front of him. He pulled the blindfold the rest of the way down and looked deep into my eyes. Then he put his arms around me and hugged me and in broken English said, "I love you."

He stepped back and said, "I meant not to kill you."

I was stunned.

He told Uli in German to tell me he had beaten me only to enforce the demand for fuel. He helped me into the front seat of the first-class section and told Uli to tell me he would untie me as soon as we were airborne.

He asked if I wanted something to drink. I nodded.

He brought me water and tilted my head back and poured it into my mouth. Then he wiped my chin with his handkerchief. He and Uli untied my wrists. I could barely lift my arms. My hands were horribly swollen.

Hitler sat down across from me and asked Uli to tell me that he too had a wife and baby girl and that they had been killed by American bombs in Beirut.

Uli brought me some cheese and a stale omelet. I ate what I could, but biting down felt strange, as if all my teeth were loose.

"What happened to the navy man?" I asked Uli.

I hadn't seen Stethem since he was led to the front, when the hijackers took my necktie to tie his hands. It was now about 10:00 at night, Middle Eastern time, about fifteen hours into the hijacking.

"He was beaten very badly, as you were," Uli said.

He was bleeding, but apparently a doctor on board had checked him, and he was recovering in the back of the plane, she said.

"We also convinced them to loosen his bindings."

Things are beginning to look better, I thought.

Uli sat across the aisle from me, talking with Hitler. He seemed very taken with her. He told her that she had saved the lives of the passengers and that he respected her. He would see that no harm came to her.

"And the other passengers, too," she kept saying.

Then—how much more incredible could this thing get?—Hitler asked Uli to sing to him, and for the next several minutes she softly sang German versions of "Patty Cake, Patty Cake" and Brahm's "Lullaby." She sounded like a mother singing to a child.

This was good, I thought, because the closer she could get to these people, the better our chances were.

Hitler asked Uli which way was east, then, kneeling on paper towels from the bathroom, both he and Crazy wailed Muslim prayers for several minutes.

Uli asked Hitler if Bob Stethem could be brought back to the front of the plane so she could tend his wounds, and he said I would have to be taken back first.

Hitler motioned for me to stand, and, with his arm around me, he led me back through the plane. The passengers kept silent. I kept my eyes forward, but I could sense terror in their faces as they looked at me.

He pointed me to a window seat at about row 17 or 18. It wasn't the same seat I was in before because my glasses weren't in the seat pocket.

Demis Roussos, the Greek singer, sat directly in front of me. He turned around, winked, and gave me a sympathetic smile.

One of the other flight attendants was in the aisle seat, chain-smoking. She offered me a cigarette. My hands were so badly swollen that it took all my fingers to hold it as she lit it for me. I noticed that my knuckles looked as if they were shifted out of place about an inch. I took four or five puffs off the cigarette and began coughing up blood. I snuffed it out.

I was exhausted and in pain, but I forced myself to stay awake. I wanted to remain alert. The hijackers were no longer brandishing grenades, but they still had the .45s. Hitler had his gun in his belt. The atmosphere seemed more relaxed.

A lot of the seats were empty. They had taken off about thirty passengers in Algiers. The airplane was a mess, littered with paper cups and food. I didn't smell too good, either. Nobody did.

I was pretty sure my spine was injured because I had a knife-point pain in the upper center of my back. My muscles were swollen and tightening, and I could only sit on the edge of my seat with my back ramrod straight.

I began to think about the emotional moment with the hijacker. His reaction had surprised me, and at the time I thought, *Family is important to these people.*

But now I was growing skeptical. "Maybe it's just a ploy, and he's planning to use me again."

I wasn't angry. My thoughts were focused on survival.

I had come to realize that these people were professionals, that they would do anything to achieve their goals. I heard later that some of the passengers who were wealthy offered them $3 million in cash. But the hijackers weren't interested in money. There was obviously a plan to all of this. They were not just a couple of fanatics out to make a name for themselves.

I had no idea who or what were the 766 Shi'ites they wanted released. But I remembered the 1,000 Arabs who had been freed by Israel several weeks before, in exchange for just three Israeli soldiers. The numbers didn't sound too bad to me.

We were still about three hours from Beirut. I could see Hitler sitting in my seat in the first-class section. He kept bouncing in and out of the seat, and I worried that my ID card would fall out of its hiding place.

It was about 2:00 A.M. when we approached the Beirut airport again. The hijackers took another one of the navy divers, a husky black man, to the front of the plane. A few minutes later, Uli led him back to his seat. He was bound and blindfolded but didn't appear to be injured. We were told to get down in the 847 position, and I could hear a lot of scurrying back and forth. I believe this is when Stethem was taken back to the front—if he wasn't already there.

The pilot came on the intercom and said the Beirut airport runways were blocked with vehicles and the lights were out. They absolutely would not allow us to land.

Uli began pulling blankets and pillows from overhead, telling the passengers to prepare for a crash landing. She looked intently at me and said, "I'm afraid we have a very difficult situation up front. Our pilot is becoming very irate with the hijackers."

"Why is he suddenly irate with them?" I asked.

"Because we have no place to land," she said. "They can't find the airport because the lights are out. We may have to land in the sea."

Chances were good that we'd all die in a crash landing, so the flight crew was no longer responding to the harassment of the hijackers.

Uli turned and walked to the rear of the plane.

I heard a shot. At first I thought they had shot one of the crew, maybe the pilot or copilot.

But then Testrake's voice barked over the intercom. "We are going in; prepare for a crash landing. We are low on fuel, and we have to land. If we can find the airport, we will land on the ground beside the runway. Otherwise, we'll have to land in the water."

Testrake sounded angry, and I feared that someone had been shot. Suddenly the plane lurched upward. I looked out the window and saw that we had skimmed a mountaintop.

Then Testrake came back on the intercom and said, "We believe the airport is just ahead, and we'll be coming in. We have fuel for only one approach."

I heard the landing gear go down. We were about to touch down when Testrake announced, "Everyone can breathe easy. They've turned the runway lights on, and they are moving the trucks. We'll have a safe landing."

Out the window I could see trucks alongside the runway. The moonlight was reflecting off the sea, about fifty meters away. If I get free, I thought, I'll have a place to go—to the water.

The plane rumbled to a stop at the end of the runway. Hitler came down the aisle, stopped, and tapped me on the shoulder. He motioned me to the back of the plane. Roussos, a blonde woman, and the four navy divers also were ordered back.

The seven of us were ordered into empty seats in the last two rows. Then the tail door sprang open, and ten or twelve militiamen ran into the plane, screaming and shouting, all brandishing automatic weapons. They seemed to be friends of the hijackers, hugging them and slapping them on the back.

Hitler pointed to the seven of us, and the militiamen motioned for us to leave the plane through the back exit. As I got off, I heard Uli begging Hitler to keep me on board.

"He is not a marine," she said. She thought they were taking us out to be killed.

Hitler grabbed at the back of my shirt as I started down the steps. One of the militiamen had me by the arm, pulling me out the door. I jerked loose from Hitler and went down the ramp.

I would take my chances on the ground. I wasn't about to get back on that airplane.

8
The Jail Cell

After the heat of the airplane, the night breeze off the Mediterranean felt good, even if we might be led off into the desert to be shot.

The seven of us were loaded into the back of a canvas-covered truck. We sat on benches, shoulder to shoulder with our captors. They were laughing and smiling, patting us on the back, and offering cigarettes.

"No one worry. We take you to American Embassy," one of them said. They all laughed. I knew the embassy was one place we were not going. I figured we were going either somewhere to be held hostage or to face a rabid firing squad. We all forced ourselves to remain calm.

"Your names?" one of the guards asked.

"Stuart Dahl," answered the oldest of the navy divers.

"Clint Suggs," said the black man.

"Ken Bowen," said the youngest of the group.

"Tony Watson," said the fourth diver, with an unmistakable Southern accent.

It was my turn. "Kurt Carlson."

"Demis Roussos, and this is my secretary, Pamela Smith," the Greek said.

"Americans?" one of the guards asked.

"Yes," I heard someone reply.

"Where in America?"

"Virginia," said Dahl.

"Indiana," said Suggs.

"Florida," said Bowen.

"North Carolina," said Watson.

"Chicago," I said. No need to try explaining Rockford, Illinois. Roussos spoke up. "I am not an American. I am from Athens."

"And I am from London," the woman said, speaking for the first time. Her accent was British.

"Do you know 'Dallas'?" one of the guards asked. "We see 'Dallas' on television. You know J.R.?"

Yes, we said, we know J.R.

The truck lurched across the airfield with a Lebanese army truck following behind as we approached a crooked and over-grown cyclone fence with a small gate.

"Be silent and put your heads down," one of the guards said, motioning with his rifle.

Two Lebanese Army soldiers stood by the gate. In contrast to the ragtag outfits of our guards, they were in full battle dress: olive green fatigues and high, black jump boots and berets. They wore pistol belts loaded with ammo pouches and canteens. They acted as if they didn't see the truck at all.

The army truck behind us stopped as we jolted onto a four-lane blacktop that circled the airport. The highway was all broken up, with grass growing three feet tall in the median. In the moonlight, I could make out the destruction that is typical of sections of Beirut. Buildings were reduced to rubble, with burned-out cars and other junk along the road. This was a real combat zone.

We were heading north, circling to the front of the airport. As we sped up a tree-lined boulevard, our driver signaled to someone in another vehicle that had a mounted .50-caliber machine gun and was parked by the stone steps of the multistory, glass-walled terminal building.

The gun-mounted vehicle pulled in behind us as we sped up the boulevard. I remember imagining that once this street must have been very impressive. Now it was a jungle of barbed wire, burned-out cars, bomb-cratered streets and sidewalks, shattered utility poles, wires, trash, and weeds. Palm and hibiscus plants that once had been well-kept grew wild.

The truck hooked a hard right, heading south onto a four-lane street that also was a jungle of overgrowth and garbage. Suddenly, the truck turned hard left, bounced over the center median and the opposite lane, dipped through the ditch, and plunged into the ghettos of West Beirut.

Careening up and down back alleys winding up the side of a mountain, the driver speed-shifted to every start and slammed hard on the brakes at every turn. Some of the hills were as steep as vertical cliffs; the turns were dizzying hairpins.

The streets were all of cobblestone or plain dirt, no wider than twenty feet, snaking between bombed-out buildings.

The only other ride I could relate it to would be an Olympic bobsled. I half-hoped that we would bounce out the back of the truck, but no such luck.

Every two blocks, we passed checkpoints guarded by young militiamen. Most of them appeared to be in their teens. They wore a mixture of French, Italian, Lebanese, Syrian, Israeli, and American military uniforms. Many wore American "Airborne" T-shirts emblazoned with skulls and crossbones, an insignia that means "kill."

They were armed to the hilt with AK-47 automatic rifles and banana clips, hand grenades, and "RPGs" (rocket-propelled grenades), .38s and .45s, and two-way radios. Some wore black baseball caps, others floppy jungle-style hats.

We passed one last checkpoint guarded by a large land cruiser and a .50-caliber machine gun, then turned off the cobblestone road and into an alley about ten feet wide.

About forty feet into the alley, the truck braked to a halt beside a block building with a bullet-pocked stucco face. It was about four stories high. The top floor looked as if it were still under construction.

We were herded into the basement through a steel door, about three feet by seven feet, with crossbracing and a small window with two bars.

The room was about twelve by twenty feet, with a high ceiling.

In the center of the room, a single light bulb hung from a wire over a wooden crate, the only furniture in the room. To the left, what was left of a shattered door—the top half—opened into another room. A third door with locks apparently led to another section of the building.

The walls were a pale blue stucco, cracked and worn; the floor was dull gray tile, dirty and streaked. My first thought was that I should have gotten back on that airplane when Hitler grabbed me by the shirt. We were probably going to be tortured to death in this room, one at a time. Uli wasn't here to hide the razor blades.

About six militiamen milled around us. They appeared to be in their twenties. They were carrying Russian-made AK-47s, Uzi automatics, and American M-16s.

One of the militiamen looked at us with a sinister gleam in his eyes and a smile on his face that made me uneasy. He unsheathed his bayonet and demonstrated a thrusting motion, the polished blade glinting in the dim light.

"I very good with this," he said in broken English. "Stick it in, pull it out, very, very good." I guess some of us must have looked a little pale, because he started roaring with laughter, as if he had pulled off a great joke. The other militiamen laughed, too. We didn't.

They motioned for us to sit on the floor against the wall. One at a time, we were led into the adjoining room, where an English-speaking militiaman with sergeant stripes on his sleeve wrote down our names, where we were from, and our occupations.

Once the interviews were finished, we were led through the door with the locks and up a stairway to the second floor, through an apartment to a corner room.

At first, no one seemed to be in charge. The guards milled about, chattering and gesturing. Then a man who apparently had authority over them arrived.

He appeared to be in his early thirties. He spoke no English but was different from the rest of the militia. He wore jeans and a sport shirt, with a .38 revolver tucked in his belt. He looked more like one of us with his fair skin, clean-shaven face, and crew cut. He glanced over his shoulder and the guards settled down. The sergeant introduced him. He was the officer in charge of the militia based in this house, a house which apparently was some sort of headquarters. He smiled and shook hands with each one of us. His name was Ali.

They call men like him "teachers." The sergeant explained that they were not only military commanders but also religious leaders. The teachers seemed to be very confident, strong-minded people. They played no games; they were more like fathers to the young, rambunctious militiamen.

The corner room was clean, with a tile floor, couches and chairs, and a coffee table in the middle. French doors opened onto a balcony. On one wall, photographs of the Iranian Ayatollah Khomeini and Shi'ite spiritual leader Imam Moussa Sadr flanked a green and red insignia. Another picture was of Dr. Shamir, whom the sergeant said was their political philosopher.

The print looked as if it had barely survived the last Israeli bombardment. It was hanging almost out of its frame, held only by one side. The sergeant said they liked it that way—it had class, Beirut-style. He said it was no more unstable than the building we were in or, for that matter, anything in West Beirut.

We sat on the couches, and the guards passed a water pitcher and cigarettes among us. We learned to drink Arab-style by tipping our heads back, holding the pitcher high, and pouring a stream of water directly into our mouths.

Several older men in their early forties, wearing jeans or military fatigues but without pistol belts or weapons, filed into the room. The guards stood back, and Ali called for someone. A young woman, who turned out to be the wife of his older brother, came into the room with hot tea for us. She was young and very polite, smiling at all of us. She wore black robes and a veil.

The English-speaking sergeant began asking again for our names, where we were from, and our occupations, comparing our answers with the notes he had taken downstairs.

"What is your opinion of your president, Ronald Reagan?" he asked.

We knew better than to praise Reagan's foreign policy in this situation, so we stuck to domestics. Stuart Dahl and Tony Watson said the president is very popular with the American people.

"His tax reforms favor the poor and middle class, the working people of our country," I volunteered.

"We hate Reagan because of his policies in the Middle East," the sergeant said. "We hate your government, but we love the American people."

Two of the older men seemed to stand out in the crowd, although they said very little except to one another. They commanded the guards with little more than a nod or a facial expression. Both were tall, about six-foot-four, and bearded. One wore military fatigues and had the air of a friendly general. The other man wore jeans and a blue knit Izod shirt. With a crew cut and studious look, he reminded me of an overaged graduate student.

They all seemed fascinated by Roussos, whose songs apparently are popular in Lebanon. They crowded around him. He spoke to them in Arabic, then told us, "Fellows, you've got nothing to worry about. You're with the Amal. You're not with the extremists, the Hizbollah."

I wasn't convinced we had nothing to worry about. I knew nothing about the Amal or the extremists, and I had just been beaten half to death by a man who said he loved me.

And now it was time out for more incongruity in this land of contradiction. From somewhere, the militiamen produced a shiny "boombox" and tuned in an Arabic rock station. Roussos went into a song-and-dance routine that had them smiling and applauding.

Abruptly, the Amal sergeant reached into his shirt and pulled out the couple's passports.

"Why do you carry American passports?" he demanded.

I could see that Roussos was in a sweat. His secretary began to cry.

"We carry all kinds of passports—Greek, American, whatever," Roussos protested. He swore he had no love for the United States.

His girlfriend, a tall, willowy blonde, nervously announced that she had no love for the United States either. She was chain-smoking Benson and Hedges.

I don't think the Amal believed their explanation for the American passports, but we were told later that Roussos and Smith would be released the next day.

Confirming my suspicions that there should have been a third hijacker aboard the plane, they were freed in exchange for one Ali Atwa, who had been arrested at the Athens airport by the Greeks. Atwa had arrived at the gate late and had gotten bumped from Flight 847.

The singer and his secretary apparently spent the night in comfortable quarters upstairs. We never saw them again.

The four navy divers and I were led back downstairs. We were given four tattered foam-rubber pads to sleep on.

As the door closed behind us, we heard the roar of a jet taking off from the airport a short distance away. We knew it had to be Flight 847.

"The hijackers must have gotten what they wanted and released the other passengers," I told the divers. "It looks as though we are the only hostages."

"That means we are military hostages; we could be in serious trouble," Stuart said.

How long would they hold us?

"Time means nothing to these people," Stuart said. "Life means nothing to them either."

9
"Afif-beb, Open the Door"

The heavy steel door closed behind us. Except for a young, English-speaking guard who seemed friendly, we were alone in the room. The guard said his name was Hassan.

My watch read 4:10 A.M. Saturday? Had it only been eighteen hours since this horror had begun? It seemed like forever.

I needed a shower badly. The odor of sweat is one thing, but the smell of sweat and fear is another. And, apparently, when I lost consciousness during the beatings, things had happened that hadn't been a problem for me since I was a child.

"Can you find me a pair of clean shorts?" I asked Hassan.

He smiled broadly, nodding rapidly. "Can do, can do," he said and disappeared through the door.

We checked out our accommodations. Two rooms, each about twelve by twenty feet, one small room about six by six with a laundry sink, and a small bathroom off the laundry room, about four by six. There were two windows, one three by three feet with wrought-iron bars and hinged wire-glass shutters, and a one-by-two-foot barred window in the bathroom. The masonry wall in the bathroom was spalling and deteriorating, probably from leaky

73

pipes. We could break through it if we had to. In addition to the single light bulb in the main room, there was an empty light socket in the bathroom.

Hassan returned with a pair of black Jantzen swim trunks with no drawstring, but they were clean.

I volunteered to try out the shower and toilet.

I heard the navy men suck in their breath when I took off my shirt. The fabric stuck to my skin where blood had spattered and dried. Hassan's eyes popped open, his chin dropped, and he said something in Lebanese. It sounded like a curse.

Speaking in English, he tried to apologize for what had happened.

"This is terrible. The person who did this to you is terrible. My teacher will punish him for this," he said.

"We ought to try to get you to a hospital," one of the divers said.

But I wasn't too thrilled about the treatment I had already received at the hands of these people. They might think that I had caused problems for the hijackers on the plane and would do the same here. A trip to the hospital might be like the trip to the embassy we were told about on the truck, and I would probably disappear into the Bekaa Valley.

"No," I said. "I'll be fine—just a few bruises."

Hassan said that he and many other militiamen had been beaten nearly to death by their enemies, the Christians and the Palestinians, and that was just part of being a soldier in Beirut.

I checked out the facilities off the small laundry room. The Turkish shower had a hole in the floor with a little ceramic ring around it that served as the toilet. The shower head was directly overhead. Apparently, the *modus operandi* here was to shower and relieve yourself at the same time, thus eliminating the need for toilet paper, of which there was none.

The shower had a hot water tank and plenty of hot water, but the faucet handles were missing. I borrowed a dime from one of the divers and used it to unscrew a handle from the laundry sink faucet, attaching it to the shower. It pays to be an engineer.

I found half a bar of soap and an empty bottle of Prell with a film of shampoo and a rag that I could use as a towel.

The spray ripped into the tender muscles of my back like the blade of a buzz saw, but after a few minutes it felt a lot better. I finished up by rinsing out my clothing and hanging it up to dry.

I sat on one of the pads and pulled my knees up and leaned gingerly against the wall.

We talked quietly. "The room may be bugged," said Stuart, who had taken some navy courses in how to react to captive situations. He was already putting his training to work.

Stuart introduced me to his fellow divers, then asked, "Are you military, FBI, CIA, or what? You have to be one or the other, or you wouldn't be here."

"Army reserve," I said.

"Good. Then the first thing we should do here is form ourselves into a military unit. That's standard operating procedure."

An E-7, or senior navy petty officer, Stuart was the divers' team leader.

"You?"

"I'm 0-4, U.S. Army major," I said.

"You're it, Major."

I was now commander of a U.S. Navy unit, locked in a stifling basement cell in the middle of someone else's war. My job was to make sure we all got home alive—no easy task, I knew. We would first need a plan of action.

"OK," I said. "We start right now figuring a way out of here. We have no idea how long they intend to hold us before killing us."

Thinking we were now the only hostages, we agreed it was unlikely that our government would try to rescue us.

"We should keep our eyes and ears open every moment. Anything at all could prove helpful," I said. "At least once a day, we will review everything we have learned and put together a plan of escape."

"We also need to work out a tapping code of some sort so that we can communicate if they happen to separate us," Stuart said.

"We'd stick out like sore thumbs and be sitting ducks out there on those streets the way we look," Ken Bowen suggested.

"If we all had beards, we'd look more like Lebanese fanatics," Tony chipped in.

"One of us is going to be noticeable even with whiskers," said Clint Suggs.

"It might help anyway," Stuart said. "Agreed then? No one shaves?" Agreed. We had no razors anyway.

"What did they do with Bob?" Ken asked.

"I heard screams and a shot," Stuart said. "I think they killed him."

"The bastards," Ken said. "Bob wouldn't have done anything to provoke them. He was one great guy and my best friend."

We didn't know for certain that Stethem was dead, only that he was not here, and the things that had happened on the plane were too ominous to be otherwise.

I told the divers I thought I had heard a shot while we were still in the air and landing at Beirut and that Uli had told me the pilot was getting angry with the hijackers.

"I figured that one of the crew had been shot," I said.

"It could have been that way," Stuart said. "But I heard several shots and screams up front in the airplane after it was on the ground. I know Bob was up front."

We talked some more about developing our plan of action. We agreed that we would work as a team and do our best to stay together. If the guards began hazing any one of us, the others would step in and help out. We would be friendly toward our captors in order to milk them for information, but we would draw lines as to how close we would get to them. Any military-type discussions with them would be strictly off-limits.

We knew that our reactions to them would be crucial to our survival. We still had a lot to learn about them, and it wasn't going to be easy. They weren't enemy soldiers, and we weren't prisoners of war. We were dealing with terrorists, plain and complicated. Some of them seemed to have the mentality of children, some seemed to have no mentality at all.

To survive and perhaps escape, we would have to be able to predict the unpredictable in a totally disorganized environment. We would have to be alert every minute to every sound and every movement. We needed to understand their motivations and the plans of their leaders better than they understood themselves.

As would always be the case, we ended the night with a prayer.

Stuart led the prayer that first night. His words burned into my mind: "Our Heavenly Father, we pray for our families, our wives, and our children. Be with my wife Martha and give her the strength to somehow deal with this situation. We pray that Bob is well. Thank you, Lord, for our lives. We have only Thee to thank for the many miracles that have kept us alive. Please be with each one of us and give us the strength and desire to survive. In His name, I pray."

We concluded with all of us repeating the Lord's Prayer. I then prayed silently for my wife Cheri. I was worried about how she was holding up, but I was sure that my family was looking after her.

We fell silent, trying to rest. But sleep was out of the question. Not only was the pain in my back growing more intense; there also was a war going on outside. The Amal kept blasting away at someone with heavy artillery. The firing continued until dawn, when it stopped abruptly.

We saw the sunrise through the window, and Stuart wandered over to look out.

"Not much happening out there," he said. He sized up our position. "The building faces south. I think the street out front runs east and west. I can see mountains to the east."

We heard another airliner take off, and from the sound we figured the airport was maybe half a mile southwest. Our escape route could take us west to the highway and southwest around the airport to the sea. We still had to learn the routine of the guards and the location and times of their street patrols and a route to the highway circling the airport.

Stuart was always thinking and coming up with ideas. "We need to ask them if we can see the Red Cross," he said.

"I doubt that they pay any attention to the Geneva Convention, but it won't hurt to ask," I said. "I would think the Red Cross should be pretty active in this part of the world."

The Geneva Convention guarantees some rights to prisoners of war, one of which is notification of government and family of the physical condition of those in captivity.

At about mid-morning, the guards brought us pita bread, baked chicken, and Pepsi-Colas and gave us more cigarettes. We sat on the floor, eating with our hands. We had no utensils. The chicken apparently was from a local restaurant. It was delicious. The Pepsi tasted great.

We spent most of the day talking with Hassan. He seemed eager to befriend us, even though he carried an AK-47 slung over his shoulder. He brought us more cigarettes and two decks of playing cards.

As we became more friendly with Hassan, we asked him to teach us some Arabic words. It seemed to please him no end that we were interested in his language. As casually as we could, we worked on words that could be useful should we have to attempt an escape.

We asked for pen and paper to write and study our newfound language, and Hassan was happy to oblige. We carefully wrote down the words we wanted to know.

"How you say, 'Open the door'?" Stuart asked.

"*Afif-beb*. Open the door, *afif-beb*," Hassan smiled.

"How about 'please'?" I asked politely. My mind was on the hijacker who had almost blown my head off, and *please* seemed like a word that might come in handy.

"*Arzjuh*, please, *arzjuh*," Hassan replied, no doubt happy to see we were interested in being well mannered.

"Family?" I pressed on, still thinking of how I had gotten some compassion from the hijacker. I was soon to discover that family is a very important concept to the Lebanese. The Amal always seemed most compassionate toward us when we talked about our families. They were always asking about our wives and children.

"Family. *Ah-a-la* means family. *Ah-a-la. Ah-a-la*," Hassan said triumphantly.

"*Ah-a-la! Ah-a-la!*" we all said in unison.

It was a good word to learn, and it was the first of many lessons we were to learn about our captors over the next several days.

10
The First Day

We rested as much as we could as the first day dragged on, talking a little bit about ourselves and our families.

I had four good men with me.

Stuart, thirty-six, had sixteen years in the navy and was in line for promotion to chief petty officer. In 1984, he was the U.S. Navy's Sailor of the Year.

All of his time in the navy had been devoted to the dive team, which is a very elite group, numbering only 100 members out of the entire navy.

He and the other divers were returning home from a mission in Greece when the plane was hijacked. They had been repairing an undersea water main.

Stuart didn't talk much about his family, saying only that he had a wife, Martha, and four children. He had a lot of personal misery to deal with during that first week. He had lost his glasses and could see only about three feet in front of him. He also had a bad case of dysentery. Nevertheless, he remained alert and on top of the situation—and we encountered many situations.

Tony was easygoing and good natured. From North Carolina, Tony, twenty-six, had two children. He and his wife, Pam, had been married during high school.

Ken, twenty-three, was single and could double for a young Tom Selleck, in both appearance and personality. He had a large family back home and a girlfriend, Becky. He liked to play the guitar and talked often about his fondest dream for the future: he wanted to buy a Jeep and cruise the beaches of Florida and camp in the Everglades.

Clint looked more like a linebacker for the Chicago Bears than a navy diver. Clint's older brother had played football with the New York Jets. Both he and Clint had played football in college at Ball State.

Clint was from Elkhart, Indiana, and grew up just a couple of miles from Notre Dame. His wife, Chantal, is Canadian and was in the Canadian Navy when they met. They have a baby boy.

At 6:00 P.M., Hassan served us a feast. His mother had prepared a large bowl of spaghetti with meat sauce along with garlic bread, whole leaves of red lettuce, black olives, cheese, pita bread, and Pepsi.

We dipped up globs of the spaghetti with pieces of pita bread. It was more food than we could eat, but I noticed that, as with the cigarettes, the guards seemed offended if we refused. After the guards left the room, we saved what wouldn't spoil and dumped the rest down the Turkish toilet.

Afterward, Hassan returned and was pleased to see the empty bowls.

We were a little nervous about the meal. It seemed too nice a gesture from people who were holding us prisoner. Perhaps it was to be our last meal.

Though our cell was stifling-hot, Hassan said we should close the wire-glass shutters to our only real window. He said they were fighting the Palestinians, whose refugee camp was just a block away. We were located on the front lines, and the Palestinians would be gunning for our building and everyone inside. A grenade could easily fit between the bars of the window.

"The mosquitoes and flies also will be less of a problem, and the rats won't be able to climb in," Hassan added.

Even with the window closed, we soon learned that the darkness of night brought out hordes of flies, mosquitoes, ants, spiders, roaches, and even a lizard.

The lizard lived beneath the ceramic ring of the toilet, but he ate roaches, so we left him alone.

The mosquitoes proved not to be a threat. They were so large that you could feel a draft from their wings just before they landed and be ready to swat them before they could bite.

Before Hassan left, Stuart told him, "We want to see the Red Cross as soon as possible."

"What for?" Hassan asked.

"We want to send a message to our families that we are OK."

"No problem. I will tell my teacher, Ali," Hassan replied.

He returned later with a notebook and pen and asked for names, addresses, and phone numbers of our families. The navy divers gave him their unit address and number, and I used my business address. We thought they might be taking it upon themselves to call our families.

That would be all our loved ones would need: a call from the Amal militia or a personal visit from a U.S. accomplice.

As we retired for the evening, Stuart recalled reading about other American hostages who were being held in Beirut, but none of us knew much about them. He thought they were marines. We all remembered the one hostage, a newsman, who had escaped from the Bekaa Valley after many months of captivity, adding to our feeling that escape might be the only hope for us.

The night brought no rest. From 7:00 to 9:00 P.M., loudspeakers in the streets blared streams of rhetoric that we couldn't understand. Hassan later explained that they were Muslim prayers mourning the dead and justifying their cause. There also were sermons exhorting the people to arms and death in the name of Allah.

As soon as the loudspeakers fell silent, the war began. We could hear land-cruisers and tanks rumbling down the street outside, the constant rattle of small-arms fire, and the thud of grenades and mortar.

We heard no screams and saw no signs of blood. Apparently no one was shooting very straight.

The hallway just outside our cell seemed to be a staging area for the battle. We could hear the guards smashing open ammunition crates and shoving cartridges into magazines and machine-gun belts.

Our building was in the direct line of fire, and we could hear the artillery shells whooshing overhead. One short round would be enough to bury us under tons of concrete.

Apparently, except for occasional harassment by the artillery, the battle stopped at about 3:00 A.M. The guards slept from 3:00 to 5:30 A.M., and we concluded that this time period would be best for our escape.

With my back and shoulders aching, I still couldn't sleep. Besides, I wanted to stay awake to keep the mosquitoes at bay. The shots I had taken before my trip didn't include malaria and hepatitis, and Stuart remembered that these were prevalent diseases here.

Hassan, sounding cheerful and friendly, awoke us Sunday morning.

"Gooooood morning, my friends."

Breakfast was served: scrambled eggs, leftover black olives, pita bread, sour cream, and hot tea.

The day passed quietly, and we used the time to clean the room. We found a crusty old towel in a corner of the laundry room and soaked it well, then scrubbed and rinsed the floor for the better part of an hour.

At about 4:30 P.M., Hassan brought us our first link to the outside world—a small portable radio with an orange plastic case.

Eagerly, Stuart dialed through the jumble of sounds and found the BBC channel from London, just after a newscast began.

What we heard left us stunned and even more concerned about our situation.

The hijackers were still holding Flight 847, which had been back to Algiers and was now, for the third time, at the Beirut airport.

The British newscaster said thirteen passengers with Jewish-sounding names had been removed from the plane during the second trip to Beirut, and twenty-six hostages—passengers and crew—were still on the plane. We had thought we were the only hostages.

The hijackers were now demanding a meeting on the aircraft

with the ambassadors from France and Britain, the International Red Cross, and Nabih Berri, leader of the Amal. Otherwise, they would blow up the plane. The hijackers claimed to have the airplane wired with explosives.

During the second stop in Beirut, the newscaster said, a man the hijackers claimed to be a U.S. marine had been killed and dumped on the tarmac of the airport. His body had lain there for two hours before being taken to a morgue in West Beirut. His identity was still unknown.

The U.S. Army Delta Team was reported to be in Christian-controlled East Beirut, preparing to join the Israeli navy in an attack to retake the airplane.

There was no mention of military hostages. Obviously, we thought, the terrorists are calling us Jewish to keep the Israelis from intervening. If thirteen people had been taken off the plane, that meant six others were being held somewhere in Beirut, but we had no idea who they might be. Other than the five of us and the Greek singer and his secretary, we were unaware that anyone else had been removed from the plane.

"The marine they killed—that must have been Bob," said Ken. "It couldn't be anyone else. Damn those bastards!"

He stalked into the other room, his fists clenched.

Later that evening, the electricity went off and the guards brought us an oil lamp and some candles. We placed them on the crate in the middle of the room, and a family of roaches ran out.

We had an unexpected visit from Ali's older brother, the tall crew-cut man in jeans and Izod shirt we had seen upstairs during the interrogations. He was with another man who, we believe, was a high-ranking officer of the extremist group, the Hizbollah.

The Izod man was calm and polite. He told us the Amal were negotiating with the hijackers to take custody of the other twenty-six hostages on the airplane.

The Hizbollah officer seemed to be irrational, ranting about Israel's killing women and children in its attacks on Lebanon.

"You were taken because Israel has taken hostages from South Lebanon. The United States must force Israel to release them if you are to be set free."

He said something about Israel's actions being in violation of "accords of the Geneva Convention," and Stuart jumped into the opening.

"Since you believe in the accords of the Geneva Convention, when do we get to see the Red Cross?" he said.

The Hizbollah man looked irritated but said nothing. The Izod man smothered a grin.

"Arrangements are being made, and within a few days—if you have not been released—you will be allowed to see the Red Cross," he said.

He asked if we needed anything and if the guards had brought us a radio, playing cards, pencil and paper, and food, as he had instructed. We were a little surprised; we had assumed the privileges we had gained were at the whim of our guards. Now we knew they had been "authorized" by the Izod man, who apparently was in command.

"How about some cigars?" said Tony.

The Izod man laughed. "Certainly," he said. "But they will have to be Dutch Masters—no Havanas. Despite what Americans think, we are not Communists and have no relations with Cuba."

The news from BBC was no better when we tuned in again at about nine o'clock. Rabin, Israel's defense minister, was saying the 766 Shi'ite prisoners would not be released without a formal request from the United States, and U.S. President Ronald Reagan was saying there would be no formal request because to do so would be giving in to terrorists. We were caught in the middle.

But the President also was saying the "first priority" was the safety of the thirty-nine hostages, and that sounded a little reassuring.

Nabih Berri was claiming he could arrange release of the 39 hostages in exchange for the 766 prisoners being held by Israel. Otherwise, he would give us back to the hijackers.

The little radio would bring us much ugly news in the days ahead. One of our worst moments was when BBC reported that 10,000 Israelis were demonstrating in the streets of Jerusalem against freeing the 766 Shi'ites. At the same time, the Hizbollah were having their own demonstration at the Beirut airport, burning American flags.

We didn't feel too happy about the attitude of the Israelis. With

The Trans World Airlines jet under terrorist guard at Beirut International Airport. Below: Television crews and reporters take their positions on the balconies of the main terminal building at the Beirut airport. The hills of Beirut rise in the background. (AP/WIDE WORLD PHOTOS)

A haggard Philip Maresca, first officer of Flight 847, talks to reporters from the cockpit of the plane. Below: An unidentified civilian is ordered by the hijackers to put his hands up as he approaches the tail section of the TWA jetliner. (AP/WIDE WORLD PHOTOS)

A view of Beirut from the vantage point of the battleship USS *New Jersey*, part of the Sixth Fleet task force. (AP/WIDE WORLD PHOTOS)

Carlson, Dahl, Suggs, Bowen, and Watson were held in Amal territory just east of the Beirut airport. (COPYRIGHT 1985 TIME INC. ALL RIGHTS RESERVED. REPRINTED BY PERMISSION FROM TIME.)

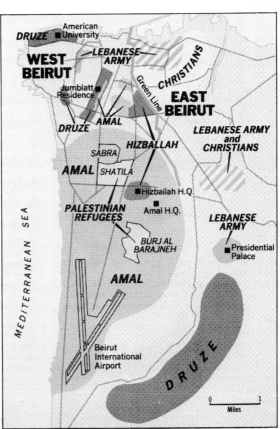

TIME MAP BY PAUL J. PUGLIESE

Hostage spokesman Allyn Conwell talks calmly to reporters at a news conference at Beirut International Airport. On his right sits Ali Hamdan, a press officer of the Shiite Muslim Amal militia, which sponsored the conference. Below: Moments later, a frustrated Conwell waves and yells as he replies to reporters' questions. Seated to his right are hostages Peter Hill and Thomas Cullins (dark shirt); Arthur Toga is at his left. The bearded terrorist in the dark shirt directly behind Cullins is the one Carlson dubbed "the Disciple." (AP/WIDE WORLD PHOTOS)

Flight purser Uli Derickson, her face showing the emotional strain of the hours aboard the airliner, speaks during a news conference held at New York's Kennedy Airport following her release. Below: One of the hooded men, who claimed to be the leader of the hijackers, addresses a rally at Beirut International Airport. Two other hooded men, believed to be the original hijackers, stand behind him, while three Shiite sheiks stand at his side. (AP/WIDE WORLD PHOTOS)

Robert Dean Stethem, the
navy diver slain during the
terrorist assault, is shown
here in a 1980 photo.
(AP/WIDE WORLD PHOTOS)

Patricia Stethem, mother of Robert Stethem, holds her hand over her
heart as her other sons, Kenneth (center) and Patrick (right), salute
while a navy honor guard folds the flag that covered Robert's coffin
during the service at Arlington National Cemetery. (AP/WIDE WORLD PHOTOS)

Bun E. Carlos, Carlson's brother and drummer for the rock group
Cheap Trick, was involved in a mysterious plan to rescue his brother.

The family—parents Vie
and Ed, wife Cheri,
daughter Meredith, and
Kurt Carlson.

FOUR-STORY BLOCK AND STUCCO BUILDING

BASEMENT

SECOND FLOOR

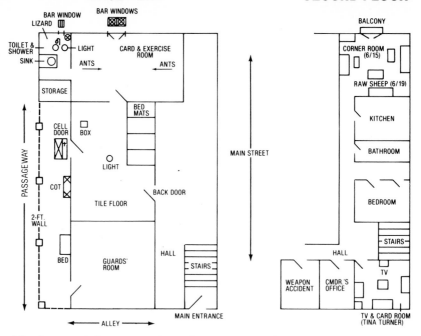

The layout of the rooms where Carlson, Dahl, Suggs, Bowen, and Watson were held captive.

Below: A scene typical of the constant war waging in the streets of Beirut. (AP/WIDE WORLD PHOTOS)

Tony Watson

Jeff Ingalls

Ken Bowen

Stuart Dahl

Clint Suggs (center), one of the navy divers held with Carlson, refuses to handle a Soviet-made AK-47 rifle offered by a Shiite Amal militiaman. Suggs, along with the other hostages, was waiting to be released and driven to Damascus. Below: Flight Engineer Benjamin Zimmermann (standing) talks to fellow hostage Rev. James McLoughlin in a Beirut schoolyard where they were awaiting their release. (AP/WIDE WORLD PHOTOS)

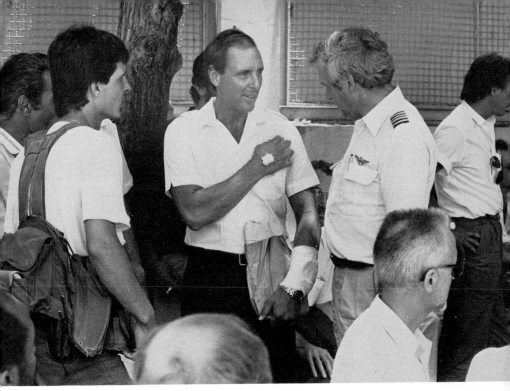

Captain John Testrake, pilot of the hijacked jetliner, talks to copilot Philip Maresca (center with bandaged hand) in the Beirut schoolyard. Below: Carrying their luggage, the American hostages prepare to board the International Red Cross cars leaving for Damascus. Kurt Carlson, who left his glasses onboard the plane, is pictured on the right wearing goggles. (AP/WIDE WORLD PHOTOS)

After spending nearly two weeks in the Boeing 727 TWA jet, Captain John Testrake relaxes in the backseat of the Red Cross car bound for freedom. Below: A Shiite Muslim militiaman, his automatic rifle stuck out of a jeep, watches the convoy of International Red Cross vehicles carrying the 39 American hostages out of Beirut and toward Damascus. (AP/WIDE WORLD PHOTOS)

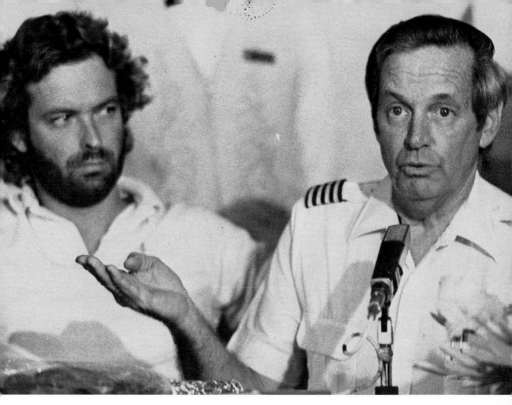

Speaking from the safety of the Syrian border, John Testrake responds to questions during a press conference. Ralf Traugott, former hostage, is seated at his side. Below: Back in Beirut, two men identified as the original hijackers were holding a press conference of their own. (AP/WIDE WORLD PHOTOS)

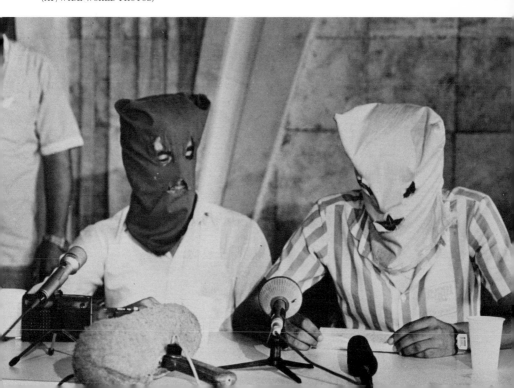

Kurt Carlson gives the "thumbs-up" sign as he and other former hostages arrive at Rhein-Main Air Base in Frankfurt, West Germany. With him are, from left, John Testrake, Blake Synnestvedt, Jeff Ingalls, and Tony Watson. (AP/WIDE WORLD PHOTOS)

Below: Kurt Carlson is welcomed home to American soil by President Ronald Reagan at Andrews Air Force Base in Washington, D.C. Kurt's wife Cheri is at his side.

Friends and family members embrace the Carlsons at Andrews Air Force Base.

A proud hometown extends a hero's welcome to Kurt Carlson as he leads the Fourth of July parade in Rockford Illinois. Cheri and baby Meredith share the celebration. (COURTESY ROCKFORD REGISTER STAR)

all the economic and military help our country has given Israel over the years, this seemed like a good time for Israel to do something for Americans.

There was another thought in the back of our minds as our second day in the Beirut jail cell came to a close. None of us said anything, but I know we were all thinking about it.

It was Father's Day.

11
Media Circus

Victory Bell is used to unusual telephone calls. As the elected alderman of one of Rockford's most bum-rapped sections of town, he has to deal with some thorny problems almost every day. And, as an assistant manager of the local telephone company, he has to solve his share of unexpected communications problems. But this was ridiculous.

"It can't be done," said Bell, rubbing sleep from his eyes. It was one o'clock in the morning.

He hung up and wearily, warily, dialed the number the voice had given him. It was long-distance, to New York.

"Do it," the voice on the other end of the line said. "No matter what it costs, do it."

Bell and the team he pulled together in the next few minutes got their picture and an accolade in the telephone company's newsletter a few weeks later, for doing the impossible.

Within two hours, they installed five new telephone lines in the home of Kurt's parents.

The telephone lines were ordered by network executives of NBC television, which had dispatched a full-blown production crew outfitted with a live-broadcast satellite transmitter to camp out in the Carlson's yard. Vie and Ed agreed to let NBC install its own phone lines.

"Our instructions were to do it without disturbing the family," Bell recalls. "I called the police department and asked them to stand by in case any of the neighbors saw us tiptoeing around the bushes in the middle of the night."

The hostage crisis in Beirut, Lebanon, had exploded into a media circus back home.

The Carlsons certainly are not recluses; they are well known in their community and exceptionally open. Local reporters doing pieces on Cheap Trick have found it remarkably easy to get around the press agents and management chain to get a direct line to Bun E. Carlos simply by calling Vie. Ed usually stays in the background, but his business reputation is high in the community, and he has been known for his years of community service as a park board member. In short, they are familiar with the media and their sometimes strange behavior.

But neither of them was prepared for what was to happen to them. They were about to become instant, worldwide celebrities.

In New York City, Mark and Kris also found that being the brother and sister-in-law of a hostage brought instant fame. New York is the nation's media capital, but except for Mark, New York's piece of the hostage crisis lacked that "hometown hook" the media seem to need to give a story something beyond governmental "talking heads."

Chicago's news media, on the other hand, were having a field day. Many of Flight 847's hostages were members of three Catholic churches in Chicago suburbs, and news helicopters buzzed back and forth between them like killer bees on the attack.

Throughout the first harrowing weekend of the crisis, Mark and Kris got constant phone calls from reporters in the New York area, but Mark decided he would talk only with CBS. "I like to watch '60 Minutes,' " he reasoned, "and I've always respected their news operation." But, more importantly, CBS was keeping quiet about Kurt's military ties.

From the U.S. State Department on down, the warning had gone out to avoid letting the terrorists aboard the plane know the names of military personnel, which, it was feared, would put them in more danger of torture or death.

CBS, anxious to keep its advantage with Mark intact, called often with information updates, even giving the couple details of what would be in the next news report long before it went on the air.

At one point, Kris joked with Mark that they never left the house anymore without first "checking out" with CBS.

Early in the crisis, the Rockford press found its hometown hook in the Chicago suburb of Algonquin, which had two Catholic priests who had pastored churches in the Rockford diocese aboard the hijacked plane.

But it could only be a matter of time before word leaked out locally, and Vie and Ed welcomed Giolitto's guidance in preparing for the deluge he knew would come. The most important thing, he cautioned them constantly, was to make sure Kurt's military affiliation was not revealed.

Vie broke into tears at the first call from a local newspaper reporter who already knew Kurt was a major in the U.S. Army Reserves.

"Please don't print it, oh, please, please don't print it," Vie pleaded, unable to hold back her tears.

To her surprise, the reporter readily agreed.

Although always open to members of the press, Vie had never really trusted them.

Her opinion changed remarkably during the hostage crisis. Not only did the first reporter guard the secret of Kurt's military status; virtually every other reporter she was to come into contact with—and there were to be dozens of them—left it alone. Kurt Carlson, Rockford businessman, was in the Middle East on business, period.

The media were themselves somewhat astounded at the story that unfolded, and the way that it unfolded, from the Carlson household. The press not only got words, tapes, reshoots, redos, cut-ins, dupes, and redupes; they also got food, telephones, and, if they needed it, a place to bunk.

Vie and Cheri would agree to any interview, so long as Kurt's military rank would not be mentioned. They appeared on "Today,"

"Good Morning America," most of the syndicated religious programs such as "The 700 Club" and "PTL," always expressing hope, always confident that, if America joined them in prayer, the hostages would come home safely.

Television cameras, press photographers, and reporters followed them to church, picturing Vie in her Salvation Army uniform, and the local newspaper headline put her optimism into a bold, upbeat headline: "I have a good feeling," it read.

There were, of course, always those reporters digging for the "real story," probing for the anger, the chance remark betraying what surely had to lie beneath the God-is-great, God-is-good stuff.

Once, NBC called Vie to set her up for a live interview with Jane Pauley and wanted to discuss with her what she would say. "I'm going to give my testimony," Vie said into the phone.

Pauley didn't think that would make the best story, the caller suggested.

"Listen, you're busy and I'm busy, so let's save your time and my time," said Vie. "The only reason I'll go on is to give my testimony for the Lord. If you don't want it, that's fine with me because 'Good Morning America' is out in the driveway right now with two carloads of people waiting for your decision. They're not happy because they got the mistaken impression I promised them an interview first. If you don't let me witness, they will, and it doesn't matter to me one way or the other."

"Everything's cool, everything's cool," the Pauley team said. "You want to talk about God, talk about God."

Cheri was interviewed once sitting alongside a talkative Middle East expert, and during a commercial break one of the floor producers suggested that she should be showing more emotion and maybe get in a few angry jabs at the Reagan administration. Cheri smiled and shrugged it off.

Mark, in New York, took a different tack, using the television cameras to project a polite but skeptical opinion of the U.S. State Department and White House response to the hostage crisis. Inside, he was furious that telephone calls from the hostages' families were never returned, and little information was shared with them. On camera, however, he stifled his anger for fear of adding to his brother's jeopardy.

But some of the press wanted anger badly. Once, a reporter for *The New York Times* called him.

"When are you going to be displeased?" the reporter asked.

"Well, if there's nothing happening on getting the hostages released in a week, talk to me then," Mark said.

The next day, a reporter from another paper called. "Did you really say that?" the reporter asked.

"Say what?" said Mark.

"*The New York Times* has a story out that says, 'Mark Carlson gives Reagan one week to get the hostages back.' "

Back home, Cheri experienced some frustrations, too. Longing for a break in the deluge of attention, she set out one day to do something normal, only to discover the meaning of a slow news day.

"Where ya goin'?" a reporter demanded, as she headed for the door.

"To take my dogs to the vet," she said.

"Oh? What're the dogs' names?" the reporter asked, digging out pencil and notebook.

Anything for a headline.

Vie took the loss of privacy in stride, insisting that the news hounds share the household as if they were part of the family. She rousted the NBC network crew from their hot and stuffy Winnebago and bunked them inside the house.

Stuart Dan, who headed the crew, became one of her favorite people. Once, during a lull in the news gathering, Dan began fingering Vie's piano, and Vie took to the organ. They both cut loose in an impromptu organ-piano duel, until one of Dan's technicians burst into the room.

"New York wants to know what the hell is going on," he said. "They say they're getting some kind of wild concert over the satellite dish."

In between taking her own phone calls, Vie took to relaying messages to Dan and other members of the media and was getting a little hoarse from shouting out names—until someone gave her a bullhorn. She still wonders what her neighbors must have thought hearing her voice blaring out messages to the television crews.

Actually, it wasn't so unusual. The whole world was shouting over bullhorns via the TV networks. Vie had sized up the situation quickly and played the media as well as she played the organ, which is pretty well.

She knew they were using her, and she was happy to oblige

because she was using them to keep the pressure on, keep the story alive, so her son wouldn't be forgotten.

She wasn't alone. Over in Beirut, the Amal were doing no less. They had the world's media on pins and needles, letting out this bit of news and that, focusing attention on the Shia, or Shi'ites, a heretofore obscure sect of Lebanese.

As the crisis ran its course on TV, everyone manipulated everyone else, and the sponsors presumably were happy with the ratings points.

12
The Guards

I spent Sunday night propped up in a corner, still too sore to sleep. Trying to rest on a battered foam mat wouldn't have been comfortable even if I hadn't been beaten up.

The other men were sound asleep. Stuart snored loudly.

After what seemed like endless hours, I started to see light coming through the doorway to the next room. My muscles were so bruised that I couldn't just pop out of bed. I rocked forward slowly, onto my knees, then fell back again. I must have resembled a boxer recovering from a knockdown punch in the last round.

Finally I was able to pull myself to my feet, and I walked stiffly, slowly, painfully into the other room.

I opened the wire-glass shutters of the window. Beirut was strangely silent, considering the bombardment we had heard the night before. I looked out the window. The sky was clear blue. The next building, under construction, was about fifty feet away. A high garden wall topped with barbed wire stood between the buildings.

I went over to the small laundry room and filled the sink with water. I removed my socks and undershorts and soaked them.

Then I showered, using the measly half-bar of soap and watered-down shampoo. I patted myself dry with the old rag and put on the bathing trunks Hassan had given me.

I rinsed out my shorts and socks and hung them on the wrought iron that covered the window. Then I sat down by the window, exhausted, but feeling a bit refreshed after the shower. The morning sun's rays coming through the window felt good on my body. It was about 7:00 A.M. That's the only thing I knew for sure.

The navy men continued sleeping, and I had some time to think. What do our captors want from us? So far we'd been treated differently from the rest of the hostages. We had been separated from the rest to die on the plane. Were we in a similar predicament here?

We couldn't escape from the airplane, but here, on hard ground, we might have a chance to get out. But first we had some serious studying to do. We had to learn our guards' routine. How bright or stupid were they? Could they be manipulated?

I took the cards and played solitaire, tuning in the radio for the 8:00 A.M. news broadcast from the BBC in London. I could always tell when the news was coming up. They played four bars of martial band music, followed by "beep, beep, beep, beep." Then an announcer said, "Greenwich Mean Time is zero five hundred hours. The morning news, as read by Richard Wilcox." I would become very familiar with Richard and the rest of the BBC newscasters during the coming week.

I hoped for new developments, something positive perhaps. But the news hadn't changed.

Outside our cell, I heard someone stirring in the passageway. Teacups were rattling. "Good morning, my friends. Is anyone here?"

It was Hassan. The navy men snored on. I called out softly to Hassan that they were still asleep.

"Do you want something to eat?" Hassan asked.

"Yes, but I don't want to disturb the others. They need the sleep," I replied.

"Well then, come outside and have breakfast with me. It's OK," Hassan said.

"Please, open the door," he added.

Opening the door required two-way cooperation. Hassan slid his key into the brass lock, which made a "clung, clung" sound as he turned it. Then I pulled back the bolt from my side of the door. The door swung open.

"Why do we have to unlock the door to let you in?" I inquired.

"In case the Palestinians come to kill you," Hassan said.

"Hassan, that's your job, to protect us," I replied.

"But I may be sleeping," he answered, putting his hand to his head in the universal symbol for sleep.

"Why would the Palestinians want to kill us?" I asked him.

"To embarrass our leaders," he answered.

"Where are the Palestinians?" I asked.

"Come, follow me," Hassan said. He motioned me toward the passageway. I peeked out the door warily before stepping out. I thought some of those Palestinians might be lurking around the corner.

Hassan led me down the outside passageway, past an old army cot where he slept, about thirty feet, to the alley. I peeked around the corner of the neighborhood apartment building. At the end of the alley, several buildings away, there was a large mound of dirt, I think twenty-five-feet high.

"The Palestinian camp is on the other side," Hassan said, pointing to the dirt mound.

There weren't any soldiers between Hassan and me and the embankment.

"Who's guarding the street?" I asked him.

"We have patrols. We only fight after dark. Boom, boom, boom!" he said, pointing his AK-47 up at the wall.

I was getting nervous about walking around in broad daylight with an Amal soldier within sight of his enemy's camp.

"Hey, you want to see my car?" Hassan asked.

"Well, how far away is it?" I replied.

"Just down there," he said, pointing down the alley.

What a mess! It was a multidented, beat-up Volvo with only one seat—for the driver. Hassan beamed proudly as I looked through the devastated interior.

As I was "admiring" Hassan's vehicle, an even stranger car wheeled around the corner. Hassan jumped and waved.

"It is my friend," he said excitedly.

This car was just a frame, with no body. But, Hassan pointed out, it was a Mercedes Benz frame.

We walked back through the passageway and sat on Hassan's cot. Hassan poured tea from a small brass pot on a tray. On the concrete, he spread a brown blanket stamped with the letters "U.S.," then yelled out, "Pistol!"

A boy of about twelve shuffled out of the guards' room, rubbing sleep from his eyes and hitching up his oversized fatigue pants. He wore a green T-shirt. Slung over his shoulder was an AK-47 almost as big as he was.

"Go get breakfast," Hassan told the boy with a smile and a wink at me.

Pistol disappeared into the guards' room and returned a few minutes later with a tray of hard-boiled eggs, some fresh pita bread, a dish of peach jam, and a block of cheese left over from the night before.

He placed the tray on the blanket, then sat down and peeled himself an egg.

Pistol and Hassan were to be our main guards. Pistol was about five-foot-six, with a boot-camp haircut and soft, sad eyes. He had a three-inch scar high on his forehead. He looked as if he had been through a lot.

Hassan was about eighteen. He was about five-foot-eleven, lean but strong, with wide shoulders. He had large brown eyes, olive skin, a straight nose, and thick, straight black hair parted on the side. He looked more like a Sicilian than an Arab.

Ken came out of the jail cell, yawning and scratching. "What's going on?"

"Wake the other guys. We're having breakfast on the patio," I said.

The others joined us, sitting on the retaining wall. Clint pointed to the building across the alley. It was yellow stucco, with large, gaping holes shot through it. It looked like Swiss cheese.

"Does anybody live there?" Clint asked.

"Yes, a family lives there. All buildings in West Beirut have families in them," Hassan said.

"Did you shoot the holes through the walls?" Clint asked him.

"No, Israeli tank did it," Hassan replied.

Pistol went back into the guards' room and returned with a fresh pot of tea. Pistol poured the tea while Hassan dumped in teaspoons of sugar, filling half of each glass. Stuart suspected that the Amal would be trying to brainwash us, and recalled that administering an overdose of sugar was one method described in his POW training. Stuart started to stop Hassan from adding the sugar until he realized that the guards were putting even more sugar in their own cups.

By now, Beirut was beginning to stir, the sun rising higher in the morning sky. In the alley, a Catholic priest and a nun walked by. They didn't look down the passageway. Then two little children, a boy and a girl, ran down the alley and peeked down the passageway at us.

"I have surprise for you," Hassan told us. He went into the guards' room and came back with a six-pack of bottled milk. The milk was imported from France and tasted like buttermilk. Nobody liked it but me. I told my fellow captives to drink it. We needed the nourishment.

When we finished the milk, Hassan tossed the empties over the retaining wall, smashing them against the neighboring building. An elderly man came to an upper window of our building and yelled something in Arabic.

Hassan leaned over the wall and shouted back to him in a defiant tone. Pretty soon the old man came walking up through the alley, toward our passageway. He wore a long gray nightshirt and had a short gray beard. He motioned to Hassan, looked over the wall, put his hands on his hips, and shook his head in disgust.

Hassan cringed. The man walked away.

"Who is that man?" Stuart asked.

"He is the father of our teacher," Hassan replied.

"Do you have a broom?" Tony asked. "If we're going to eat outside again, we'd better clean up this mess."

Hassan sent Pistol to get one. It had about eighteen inches of handle and six inches of straw left on it.

Using a piece of cardboard as a dustpan, Ken and Tony cleaned up the glass and assorted other trash. There was enough to fill a dumpster. We piled up the garbage in a heap in a corner, as neatly as we could.

Just as we finished our cleaning detail, Hassan heard footsteps down the street. We didn't hear them, but Hassan had a keen sense of hearing for strange sounds.

He bolted up and ran out the passageway, around the corner into the alley. By the time we looked up, Hassan had returned.

"Go back inside, please," he urged us, motioning us back to the door.

Pistol straightened up, too. We hustled back to our cell, where we stayed the rest of the day.

Clint, Ken, and Tony napped on the foam pads while Stuart and I played cards in the other room. Stuart had his own version of solitaire and won every game. When he was bored with winning, Stuart staged war games on the floor of our cell—Black Ants against Red Ants. He would throw a dead fly or a roach into the middle of the room and watch the ant armies flow from the crevices in the walls, converging in a massive Battle of the Bugs. Soon we both tired of cards and ants, and talked about our security.

We must keep the two doors locked at all times, we decided. Windows, too, at night. We set up a guard detail to make sure one of us was always awake at night. I told him I'd be on guard until I got too tired. I didn't figure on getting much sleep; I was still too sore.

At about 1:00 P.M., Hassan came to the door and knocked.

"Time to eat," he said, opening the door. With him was a guard we hadn't seen before. He had short, blonde hair, stood about five-foot-ten, and had freckles. He looked more English than Middle Eastern.

"I want you to meet Hassan, your new guard," said the Hassan we knew. "You're not leaving us," I protested.

"No, no. After we eat, I need to go home and sleep," he said.

The new Hassan sat down and had lunch with us. It was cream cheese, pita bread, and peach jam. It was good, and we chowed down.

"We will call you Hassan II," I said to the blonde guard. He smiled and said, "OK." He spoke reasonable English, but not as well as Hassan I.

I figured the Arabs must not have a lot of names they can name their babies, so a lot of people have the same first name. It can be confusing. Then again, our names confused them.

Before leaving, Hassan said we should have Arabic names. I asked what my name would be.

"You are Hassan." Great, I thought, another one.

Then he pointed to Clint and said, "You are Mohammed."

He looked at Stuart, saying, "You are Ali."

To Tony, he said, "Ahkmed."

Then they turned to Ken, and both Hassans laughed.

Hassan whispered something into Hassan II's ear, and they shrieked and rolled on the floor.

"OK, what's my name then?" asked Ken.

"You will be called Girlie, because you have many girlfriends. Girlie, girlie, girlie!" they repeated, convulsed in laughter.

"How many girlfriends have you? Two, three, ten?" asked. Hassan.

"Just one," Ken said. Then he winked at them. "One at a time."

Hassan left, his laughs echoing down the hall. "Good-bye, my friends," he called.

After lunch, Hassan II worked on his English with Tony, and Tony tried to learn Arabic from him. He taught Tony how to count in Arabic. Tony asked Hassan II about his school years and his family. Tony was very patient with Hassan's broken English and compared some of Hassan's experiences to his own. Hassan was intrigued with Tony's early marriage at age 16. He said that Lebanese men cannot afford to get married until they are about 35 and can support many wives. Tony and Hassan sat in the corner and talked for hours while the rest of us played cards.

The afternoon dragged into the evening. Around seven, young Pistol returned with our dinner—chicken and fries again, in paper carryout bags with Arabic letters and red chickens. It was good.

After dinner, we heard a truck drive up the alley. We got anxious as we heard strange voices. It sounded like four or five people.

Hassan II opened the door and talked to the voices.

The strange guards were dressed in camouflage battle fatigues and wore black T-shirts with "Airborne" emblazoned on the front, with skull and crossbones. American marine shirts, I thought. These weren't guards; they were Amal militiamen from a different unit in another part of town.

They came into the room.

"One at a time, come with me," Hassan II said.

"What for?" we asked nervously.

"We have your belongings." I believed him.

Stuart went first. He was away about thirty seconds, then returned, duffel bag in hand.

The guards ordered Stuart to empty the contents onto the floor.

Stuart had his civilian clothes, books, paper, his shaving kit, and his exercise wheel. It's like a little wagon wheel with two hand grips. The guards picked it up and puzzled over it, scratching their heads.

"Exercise wheel," Stuart told them. "Here, let me show you." He then proceeded to roll around the floor with the wheel, kind of pushing up his body with it.

The militiamen then tried it, but all fell flat on their faces. Hassan II was able to work the wheel, after considerable effort. They roared with laughter.

The others went out, one at a time, and each returned with a duffel bag. Clint had a pair of jump ropes in his bag. Clint showed them how to jump, and they had a go. It looked bizarre—men in combat boots and AK-47s strapped to their sides bouncing up and down with a jump rope.

Ken noticed his radio missing from his bag. The guards didn't know where it was, they said.

All the divers had green fatigues and jump boots in their bags. They were confiscated.

I was the last to go. "I am not military and have no duffel bag," I told the guards, who had two bags left—those of Jeff Ingalls, another diver, and Bob Stethem.

Stuart explained the bags were not ours.

"These bags belong to the man who was killed on the airplane," Stuart said, hoping to prevent our captors from realizing that they'd left one military man on the plane.

"We are sorry. Take what you want for his family," a militiaman replied.

I was out of luck. No luggage. Ken loaned me a pair of jeans and a white T-shirt. Stuart gave me an extra pair of underwear and some socks.

Finally we had soap, toothpaste, shampoo, and clean towels. We hid the razors and shaving cream.

Then the militiamen left. Hassan II stayed with us. By now it was 8:00 P.M. The grandfather came down to see us, entering through the back door. He motioned us upstairs. Hassan II went along. The old man brought in a tray of cups and Turkish coffee. Hassan II dealt cards, then ran into the adjacent room. He returned with a bowl of cinnamon balls.

We ate them and drank the coffee, which tasted like espresso— very strong.

The windows were wide open, and a cool breeze wafted over us. It felt wonderful. My lungs opened up. I could breathe again.

At 10:00, Ali, the teacher, came in, smiling as he greeted us with *"Salaam ale com."* We returned the greeting with *"Ale com salaam."*

He spoke with Hassan II, who then told us, "You will go to bed now."

He led us back to our cell. Ominous sounds filled our ears: boxes of ammunition being broken open on the concrete, guns being loaded—war sounds.

We fidgeted with the radio, listening for the BBC. A truce had been signed that day, the radio said, between the Amal militia and the Palestinians.

Could the BBC be wrong? We were soon to learn that in Beirut a truce doesn't always mean the end of the shooting. Sometimes they take a couple of days to spend all their ammunition. Usually truces don't occur until the leaders take away their soldiers' weapons, we discovered.

Tonight's truce would be loud. We heard machine-gun fire in the alley, mortar sounds, big booms. I told the guys I hoped they didn't hit the building next to us. It was taller, and I feared it would tumble down on us.

We settled down to another fitful night amid West Beirut at war.

13
Sing Along and Duck

Tuesday morning, we were awakened with a start as guards burst into our room. I thought we were headed for sudden death.

"Down, down, everyone, stay down," one guard shouted. "There is a sniper on the roof of a nearby building," he told us. The sniper was a Palestinian, the guard said, who was trying to kill Ali, one of the Amal teachers, and also wanted to kill us. The Amal's mortal enemies, the Palestinians, knew right where we were. That gave me no comfort.

But this Palestinian was not to have a good day at all. Amal militiamen soon had him surrounded, and they led him off the roof of the building, into the house in which we were captives. He was placed in the guards' room next to us, and we were brought in to watch some frontier justice, Beirut-style.

Hassan tied his hands beneath his legs and used one of our pillows to wedge him up on a shelf four feet off the floor. They began punching and slapping him ferociously. One of the guards offered us a gun. "Here, take this. He was going to kill you, so you may kill him. Kill him before he kills you."

"No," we replied, shaking our heads vigorously. We wanted no part of this grizzly scene.

103

We raced back to our room. We were really uptight. If this is how they treat the folks in the next block, God knows what they might try on us, we thought. The whole scene was beginning to remind me of one of those postapocalyptic movies that take place in New York, with territories controlled by vicious gangs. This Palestinian may have just wandered off his gang's turf, for all I knew.

Back in our room, we sat down, relieved to be away from the torture scene. The grandfather who lived in the house tried to calm us, then led us upstairs for breakfast.

"You to have special treat," one of the guards said as the old man smiled and nodded. The meal was one of their real delicacies.

It was a plate of raw sheep parts. There were chunks of heart and liver, which looked like bits of steak. The flesh was white and fluffy. The grandfather showed us how to eat the parts. They were to be dunked first in a bowl of salt.

We gulped, but dared not refuse his gesture, because these people seemed to take drastic measures if they were insulted.

We all ate the raw sheep parts. The flesh tasted rather like popcorn, I thought. At least nobody got sick from it. We smiled and thanked him. He seemed pleased. He liked us. After all, we'd cleaned up the passageway behind his house.

The guards who had joined us for the feast motioned us over to the balcony. Amal militiamen were throwing the beaten Palestinian in the trunk of a car. He was screaming, pleading for his life, and praying to Allah. Somehow, I don't think he is still among the living. As the Palestinian was driven away, our guards praised Allah and said a few prayers.

Later that day, I saw another example of frontier justice. Beirut has a police force, but because of the anarchy there it has little authority. Therefore, if you need some law enforcement, you ask the local militia and reward them with a gift.

A well-dressed local businessman came, with a box wrapped in gift paper. It was for the grandfather, he said. We thought it might be a bomb. "No," said Hassan, "the man has had his car stolen by a Palestinian. He wants the Amal to get the car back for him, and the man who stole it."

I imagined the fate of the car thief, should he be caught. All of this was beginning to make the *Godfather* movies look like "The Muppet Show." We were, in fact, in a real-life gangland situation. It was gruesome.

Hassan left with the present and we sat down on our beds, reminiscing about home. Whenever Clint talked, he smiled, and tried to draw us all into his memories of home. He remembered some good times in Chicago—Christmas shopping in the Loop, the Field Museum, Wrigley Field and the Chicago Cubs. We were all Cub fans and discussed baseball for awhile. Clint rolled up a newspaper, and Ken balled up some aluminum foil. We spent the afternoon throwing curveballs and hitting home runs. Clint brought us closer together and was responsible for a few of our happy moments.

It was 6:00 P..M. when our guards brought us a meal of rice, chicken, beef, boiled potatoes soaked in butter, and some leftover French milk, which was beginning to thicken. I enjoyed it—it beat raw sheep.

After dinner, Hassan led us out of our cell. We sat on the retaining wall in the passageway. Ken had seen a guitar when we had breakfast upstairs and asked Pistol if he could use it.

Ken had wrestled with the guitar for a while, trying to tune it— a task he finally accomplished. It probably hadn't been played since the Amal began devoting all their efforts to clobbering Palestinians.

Ken could play all right, but he couldn't sing at the same time. Tony and Clint could also pick a bit. So, all afternoon we rehearsed some tunes, and our guards were intrigued by the music. By the time evening came, we were ready. Outside on the wall, we let loose.

Clint did a soulful rendition of "House of the Rising Sun," a song about people trapped in another kind of prison—a whorehouse in New Orleans that's "been the ruin of many a poor boy, and God, I know I'm one." Altogether appropriate, under the circumstances. Since the hit version was done by the Animals, and since we were kind of like caged beasts in Beirut, we decided that we'd call ourselves the "Beirut Animals."

We switched to folk music and harmonized to the sixties song "Michael Row the Boat Ashore." Another irony, I thought, when we sang the line "The River Jordan is chilly and cold." That river couldn't be more than a hundred miles away from here, I figured.

We didn't sound bad, and our guards enjoyed the show. Come to think of it, I suppose we should have done "Jailhouse Rock."

Our guards didn't seem concerned that we'd be noticed; they were tapping their feet to the music. I wondered if we could play ourselves out of captivity. Perhaps we'd be the house band at Nabih Berri's headquarters.

The Amal chaplain and the tall Izod man we had met briefly on Sunday heard our music and joined the guards.

The chaplain had stringy red hair, a red beard, and the weathered face of a windblown fisherman. Linking his looks to his role as a religious leader, I mentally nicknamed him "the Disciple." He was intensely nervous, chain-smoking Winstons and constantly rolling a set of worry beads between his fingers. He spoke little English but seemed to strain to hear everything said around him. He often frowned at the childish antics of our guards.

Our music seemed to please the Disciple and the Izod man; they smiled and nodded along. From the look on his face, I knew the Izod man was familiar with our songs. When the impromptu concert ended, we found out why he knew so much about our culture.

He was no longer wearing the designer shirt and jeans but was dressed in military camouflage fatigues and a green T-shirt. He spoke English like an everyday American. He told us he had lived in California for seven years. He told us to call him "Joe." That was all, just "Joe."

Joe sat down on a wall, next to Ken. I asked Joe, "When are we going home?"

"Possibly a few days or longer. Don't worry, though; the Shia are very patient people. As soon as the Israelis agree to release the Shia prisoners, you will be released."

Ken asked if we would ever be turned back over to the two hijackers. We had heard on BBC that Nabih Berri, the Amal leader, said that, if negotiations broke down, we might be turned over to the pair.

"No, no," Joe laughed. "They are no longer here."

We breathed a sigh of relief. Clint smiled.

"But they were good boys," Joe said. "It was not easy for two young men to control an aircraft and 153 people. If they had failed, everyone could have died." Joe said they were under extreme pressure because a third man was supposed to get on the plane to help them. Joe left us with the impression that the hijacking had been planned carefully.

He didn't mention the killing of Robert Stethem, and we weren't about to ask.

"Also, I'm sure you'll not be on that airplane, because we understand that it is in poor mechanical condition and unsafe to fly. You may have to fly back on Middle East Airlines."

No thanks, I thought. I'll take a canoe.

"Do any of you know much about the situation here in Lebanon?" We didn't.

"Beirut was once the crossroads of the Middle East.

"There are nineteen religious sects in Lebanon," he said. "The Shia are the largest, with 1.6 million people. From these people, we have many young men who want to fight, so our Amal militia is strong. We presently are rearming, as the Israelis destroyed or confiscated nearly everything of value in West Beirut.

"Each religious sect has a radical wing, including the Christians," Joe continued. "The Shia have the Hizbollah, who live in the south suburbs of Beirut and in the far eastern villages of the Bekaa Valley."

So, the hijackers were Hizbollah, I figured.

"The remainder of our Shia people live in the south of Lebanon. They are rural people. They are the hostages that Israel is holding, farm people, men, women, and children. Your own government has condemned them for taking these people prisoner."

"Are any of you Jewish?" Joe asked. We froze. All the terror of the flight came rushing back.

"Relax, don't fear me. Understand, we have nothing against Jews or any other nationality. We only hate their leaders, the Zionists, whose sole purpose is war, to destroy and conquer."

Joe continued his history lesson. "When Israel first invaded south Lebanon, my people welcomed them. They said they had come to rid the land of Palestinian terrorists. We thought that was fine. But then they advanced into Beirut and the Bekaa Valley.

For weeks they bombed West Beirut with their artillery, air force, and navy. West Beirut, as you see, is home to many of us, not just Palestinian refugee camps. Many Shia died.

"With the help of the Christian Lebanese, who live in East Beirut, the Israelis planned to destroy Muslim opposition and install a Christian puppet government, which they could control."

Joe said the land where the Shia live in West Beirut, near the airport, was government-owned. The Shia, Lebanon's poorest people, built their houses there. They were squatters and had nowhere else to go. Bashir Gemayal, the Christian president, wanted to bulldoze the Shia neighborhoods out of existence and move the people into refugee camps. He told the Americans he was a moderate who had support from us and other Muslim groups.

"But he had no Muslim support and was soon killed. Then civil war erupted again. Your marines were killed when they tried to join in the fighting. It was not your war. You know nothing of our struggles. The building where your marines died is less than a quarter-mile from here. It is not only Americans who have died, you know. Thousands were killed by Israeli rocket bombs and cannon fire. Thousands more were killed in our civil war."

"When will it all end?" I asked Joe.

Joe stared at me, silent for a few seconds. He didn't know when the end to the fighting would come. I wondered how many friends and relatives he had lost to the killing. He looked down. He didn't answer my question; he obviously couldn't.

I began to think that, although I was getting a one-sided view from Joe, it was a side I hadn't heard before.

Joe asked if any of us knew before about the Shia the Israelis were holding in Atlit. We answered that we did not.

"You see, you will never read anything about it in your papers or magazines, about the 766 hostages the Israelis have taken out of Lebanon to prison in Israel.

"Despite the many problems here, the people of Beirut believe in a central government. We all pay our taxes to support the schools, the roads, the utilities, and the Lebanese army. What we are fighting for is political power and a democratic form of government, where the majority rules. In such a government the Shia would have political power. We've had none in the past.

"We laugh at the Americans who call us Communists. We are

very much anti-Communist. Ha! In that system, a small number of people are wealthy and rule, and they oppress everyone else. I lived in California for seven years, and the American form of government works.

"Our present government is no government at all. The government has not had a cabinet meeting since April.

"The only man who respects the government ministers' titles is the doorman of the presidential palace."

I decided to ask him something that was still bugging me. The Shia had pictures of the Ayatollah Khomeini all over the place, and I had it in the back of my mind that we might be shipped off to Iran if we became too hot for the Amal to handle. So I just came out and said, "Will we be going to Iran?"

Joe smiled. "Let me tell you about why we honor Khomeini. He is our spiritual leader. But the Iran government has far different interests than we, and they don't want any involvement in Lebanon. We don't want them here, either. We are interested in his spiritual teaching only."

"Iran believes in conquering all of the Arab states to set up one Muslim country. The Amal believe in national sovereignty."

This was interesting, to be sure. But I had more important things on my mind.

"How are the negotiations for our release going?" I asked Joe.

"Don't worry yourselves with the negotiations. Think only about your families and the day that you will be rejoining them. Now we can only wait and pray to our God. I am sure that he will prevail for both of our concerns."

Joe then handed us some newsmagazines he'd brought in with him.

"Here, read all about yourselves," he said with a grin. "I got these from Middle East Airlines."

Then he turned around, bade us good night, and walked down the alley.

Hassan said it was time to get back to our cell. Once there, we talked for a long time about Joe.

He had eased our minds considerably. Here was an intelligent man who knew what was going on. He seemed like a reasonable enough guy.

I mentioned the marines—the ones Joe said had been caught in the crossfire. More than 200 of them had been killed, not in battle, but in their barracks, by a bomb. Those were the tactics of cowards, we agreed. That took a lot of our sympathy away, and we also remembered that these were the same people who, if they didn't plan it, at least didn't try to stop the hijacking of Flight 847 and the killing of Bob Stethem.

The fact that one American had died would also take away the sympathy of the majority of the American people. We had not understood the Shia people, but neither did they understand us.

Before turning out the lights for the night, we leafed through the magazines.

"Well, Joe was wrong about one thing," I said while looking through the magazines, all American.

"What's that?" Clint asked.

"He said we would never read about his people in our press. But here it is, telling about them."

Since we had nothing else to do, we read about Joe's people.

The Amal movement was begun in the 1960s, by Moussa Sadr, a Shi'ite holy man who went to Iran for his religious training. When he returned to Lebanon, he began to unite the Shi'ites, the lowest of Lebanon's Muslim sects, who had been pushed around the country by the Christians, the Sunni Muslims, and the Druse Muslims, who, in an unholy alliance, ran Lebanon for decades after the country was carved out of Syria by the French in the 1940s.

Sadr went to Libya in 1978 and has not been seen since. Some people consider him a martyr; some think he is still alive. The Lebanese Shi'ites have no love for the Libyan strongman Moammar Khadafy because many believe he is responsible for Sadr's disappearance.

After a period of jockeying for position, Nabih Berri gained control of the Amal Shia. He was a lawyer, whose ex-wife and children call Dearborn, Michigan, home. Many Shi'ites and other Lebanese groups live in the Detroit area.

The Hizbollah, or "Party of God," are the radical Lebanese Shia, who long for the kind of extreme Islam practiced by the Shi'ites in Iran under Khomeini.

While we were there, it seemed as if the Shia had finally made it, controlling a good portion of Muslim West Beirut. But how long could they hold out?

Syria is said to exert a great deal of influence over the Amal, the Shi'ite political and military establishment in Lebanon. Israel to the south wants the Amal crushed, Joe said, and wants the Maronite Christians to take over.

The Sunni Muslims, more moderate than the Shia, would like Beirut to return to its former position as the Middle East's financial center. Other radical fringe groups such as the Hizbollah want to set up an Islamic Republic, as Khomeini has done in Iran.

The day had been eventful, to say the least—everything from raw sheep to beaten Palestinians, a lesson in Middle East politics and a gospel music concert for Muslim militiamen.

It was about 9:00 P.M. We were not quite ready to settle down, so we tuned in the BBC "World News." Demis Roussos and Pamela Smith had been released, the announcer said. President Reagan said he would make no concessions to the hijackers, the news continued.

Now some good news. Reagan said he had asked the International Red Cross to mediate in the situation. A meeting would be set up in Israel.

Then the bad news. The BBC commentary segment noted the Red Cross did not trust the Israelis because of their actions during previous hijackings. The Israelis didn't trust the Red Cross, saying they had violated some article of the Geneva Convention. It seemed nobody trusted anyone in this part of the world.

I switched off the radio. "Come on guys, this is just politics. I'm sure they are working behind the scenes to make some kind of deal, a settlement so everyone can save face. Lights out."

I thought we'd sleep soundly. The truce was in effect, and the Amal and the Palestinians had both gotten in their last licks—we hoped. Now, an eerie silence fell over Beirut. We'd gotten used to bombs going off and to rifle fire. It became background noise, as if we were staying in an apartment adjoining one of Chicago's el tracks, with clanking trains rumbling by at all hours of the day and night. Human beings can get used to just about anything, even constant warfare.

The quiet was not to last. We heard Hassan's beat-up Volvo, which had no muffler, roaring through the neighborhood. Then someone came clomping down the passageway to the door of our basement cell. It was Hassan, with a sheepish grin on his face.

"Uh, I need some help, guys." We got up from our pads. Hassan, it seems, had been celebrating two events: the truce with the Palestinians and the end of Ramadan, the Muslim holy month. He was doing something that reminded us of youngsters in America; he was hot-rodding his jalopy up and down the alley near our house. Unfortunately he'd jumped the curb and couldn't back the car off it.

Ken, Clint, and Tony shook their heads and followed Hassan outside. Just as they got to Hassan's rolling wreck, they found out that a Beirut truce is about as reliable as a used-car salesman's pitch. Shots rang out as the men began lifting up the car. Hassan engaged his rifle and began firing back. Ken, Clint, and Tony gave a heave-ho, lifted that car off the curb in about two seconds, and then got the hell out of there. They ran madly back to the house, down the stairs, and into our cell, where we locked the door.

We heard Hassan's car roar back down the alley as the gunfire stopped. Shortly, we heard the "clung, clung" of Hassan locking our door. That was the last noise I heard. I slept soundly for the first time in many nights.

14
"Mitzi mitzi beshi beshi"

Wednesday morning we awoke at about 9:00, and the guards brought us breakfast. Hassan thanked us for our rescue of his car. Then the divers did calisthenics. Clint demonstrated his great strength by doing eighty push-ups. The guards were a little intimidated by his display of strength, because they had been acting very macho, strutting around and playing the big-shot role. Clint's strength was quiet but formidable.

We tried to get the guards to do sit-ups, but they didn't know how. Through the workout, I just sat in the corner on my little pillow; my back was still much too sore to exercise. I wished I could have, though, to relieve some of my tension. At home, a good workout refreshed me for my day at work, and a workout here would help me to face imprisonment in a better frame of mind.

The guards came in a bit later with morning newspapers. Pictures on the front pages showed Palestinian and Amal leaders embracing because of the truce.

That afternoon we worked on our Arabic lessons with Hassan and Pistol. We had advanced to phrases like, "Good day, my good friend," "Praise Allah," and "Where is the sea?" Our vocabulary was now up to about fifty words.

113

We whiled away some time playing poker—five-card draw, seven-card, and blackjack. Stuart and Ken constructed a pipe from aluminum foil and smoked their own Beirut blend . . . cigarette tobacco mixed with leftover dried tea leaves. Hassan tried it and gagged. "Please. Please. Let me buy you pipe tobacco."

Hassan had a great personality. I think he'd been instructed to keep our spirits up. Sometimes he would come in, notice we were just sitting there staring or looking glum, and shout, "Hey, let's play cards!" And we would. Another time he came in laughing and started doing acrobatics—standing on his hands and trying to walk around the room. The navy divers got into the act, too. I was still feeling too much pain to do anything but watch this wild scene of Hassan, Clint, Stuart, Tony, and Ken all trying to walk around on their hands.

Our young guard was a good soldier, not careless with his weapon, as were so many of the others. He spoke reasonable English. He needed a larger vocabulary and some practice, and we provided him with an opportunity to improve his language skills.

Hassan told us he had served nearly two years in the militia and wanted to return to school. He was glad the truce had been declared, he said.

We also liked Hassan because he brought us Marlboro cigarettes. Tony asked him once if he had any Lebanese cigarettes. Hassan grimaced and explained, "Only the Christians smoke those. We are Marlboro men." It was true: ads for those cigarettes were everywhere in West Beirut. On billboards, on television, in full-page newspaper ads, there he was, the Marlboro Man. I would say Marlboro Man posters outnumbered Khomeini posters at least ten to one.

Since the truce was on, the Amal no longer hated the Palestinians—at least for a while. Lebanon is such a small place, with so many warring groups, that practically everybody knows one another or is somehow related. Late in the afternoon Hassan brought in two men dressed in spiffy combat gear, with new boots, new weapons, and olive berets. "These are my friends from school," he said. Both wore buttons that bore the number thirteen and the words, in English, "Palestine Liberation Organization.

Take me to American University Hospital." A couple of days before, Hassan had probably been lobbing grenades at these guys or at least at their buddies. Now they were the best of friends again. I thought back to my American history lessons, to stories of our Civil War, in which the Union and Confederate soldiers would kill each other by day, then sneak off into the woods together at night to drink whiskey and play cards.

"Tell them your new names," Hassan said, pointing to each of us in turn. We played along.

"I am also Hassan," I said.

"Mohammed," said Clint.

"Ali," said Stuart.

"Ahkmed," said Tony.

Ken said nothing but gave Hassan an exaggerated wink.

"Girlie!" Hassan shouted gleefully. He and his pals roared with laughter.

Hassan told them what part of the U.S. we were from. They didn't speak English but were excited to see real, live Americans. They gestured with their hands, and both spoke at once to Hassan. He laughed.

"They said to tell you they have relatives in Los Angeles, and they want to go there," Hassan told us. These, then, were the rabid, anti-American soldiers of the PLO. Down with America, and take me to Tinseltown! Hassan, too, told us he wants to get the fabled green card to come to America and work at his trade, carpentry.

It seemed as if all of West Beirut was headed to Los Angeles. I thought maybe I'd better phone Mayor Tom Bradley and warn him to expect several hundred thousand visitors who liked to shoot at each other with automatic weapons.

L.A. was a more popular destination than Iran or Damascus. The electricity worked all the time, and besides, Beirutis already know the names of all the freeways, from television shows.

Hassan told us about his family. He had a father much older than his mother. He explained that Shia custom allows a man to have more than one wife, but he didn't say if his dad had more than one. He had many brothers and sisters. He had an older brother who had been killed in the fighting. It was a good family, he told us.

Pistol was very obedient to the older guards, even though they constantly teased him by boxing his ears, throwing hard-boiled eggs at him, and tripping him up. He was the low man on the totem pole, and he told us he was anxious to get back to school. Pistol was a good little soldier. He told us his father was in America—a captain in the U.S. Army.

So I suppose someday he too will come to L.A.

In addition to our guards and their friends, we were often visited by members of the militia. Not all of them were as nice as Hassan and Pistol, though. Some professed a violent hatred of everything American and liked to play games with us, sometimes for humiliation. They took great delight in coaxing us to repeat Arabic phrases that we didn't understand and which they never bothered to explain to us.

One was "*mitzi mitzi, beshi beshi.*" They especially loved to have Clint say it, and they made him say it over and over. Later we found it was a phrase from one of their childhood nursery rhymes. Occassionally Clint would turn the tables and ask them to repeat phrases like "I want to be an airborne ranger, I want to live a life of danger." The militia also enjoyed sitting with us and smoking cigarettes, blowing the smoke straight up to the ceiling, as if it represented some magnificent feat.

They took sinister delight in playing a game with us, a form of Russian roulette. They'd tap the magazines of their weapons as if to lock them on automatic, pull back the bolt, aim at us, and— click. If we complained, they would laugh and point the guns at each other or at the ceiling.

The trick, apparently, was to tap the magazine only partway into the load position and not place a cartridge in the chamber. But their guns were old, and they didn't clean them, so sometimes a cartridge would slip into place and the gun would fire. Once, one of them shot his own buddy, through the shoulder, and they rushed him to the hospital.

Three of the more reckless militiamen were nothing less than bona fide thugs. That's the only word I can think of to describe them. They were Kamel, Farisch, and Afif, three stooges I never want to see again. From the beginning, we felt they really hated us.

Kamel, a short, fat fellow, was a Palestinian, but a member of the Amal militia anyway. He'd try to humiliate us in front of his comrades. He'd point his gun at us and say, "Tomorrow, boom-boom-boom." But the other guards didn't see any humor in that.

We didn't either.

Farisch was like the tall hijacker on the airplane—a little bit crazy. In fact, the other guards called him "Crazy" and told us not to pay any attention to him. We had to pay attention to him because we felt he was a threat to our lives. For a while, we kept smiling at his antics in order to survive.

Afif was Lebanese but looked and spoke French. He was the type who would talk nicely to you while stabbing you in the back. He told the others he was trying to make fools of us. We didn't trust him, either.

Kamel settled down after I did him a favor, though. He said he had a girlfriend named Therese, who was English and was living in southern Lebanon. Could I write her a letter? Well, sure, I'd be happy to.

I wrote a somewhat standard "darling dearest" letter and asked Therese to marry Kamel and all that sort of blather. Stuart suggested I sabotage the letter by suggesting Therese commit strange acts of sexual intrigue, but I demurred and kept it straight. What if the letter was a test? What if Therese was a KGB agent with poisoned-tipped darts? No, "darling dearest" the letter remained.

Wednesday night, the thugs were in a Three Stooges mood, playing all sorts of unpleasant games with us. After tiring of the gun game—"Click, boom-boom, ha-ha"—they got into a wrestling match with each other. Then our wristwatches caught their eye, and they asked what they cost. I said $200; the divers said $100. They took my watch and gave me a cheap dimestore ring, representing the exchange as a fair trade.

Ali got word of what was going on, warned them to knock it off, and returned my watch. He took us upstairs and told us we were to watch a videotape on his VCR.

Stuart warned us before Joe inserted the cassette, "This is probably some sort of propaganda tape, to convert us to their viewpoint."

The tape rolled. It was propaganda, no doubt about it.

It was a Tina Turner special. We watched Tina strut across a stage, singing "What's Love Got to Do with It?" as we ate ice cream served up from the Beirut version of Baskin-Robbins.

We were on a mental roller coaster. A short time earlier we thought we'd be shot by the thugs. Now we were being treated to ice cream and Tina Turner.

The three thugs returned again, though, and stole Clint's watch. That did it. We complained to Ali when he returned. He looked annoyed and promised, "You'll never see them again." We didn't. And Ali brought back the watch.

15
The Press Conference

Early in the afternoon, Thursday, June 20, we were sitting on our dusty mattress pads, engrossed in a poker game. We were competing for beans. Clint and Ken were cleaning up, winning all the beans.

Hassan came to the door and peeped in at us. "Please, open the door," he said.

I got up and let him in.

Two men came into the cell with him. Hassan was not his usual friendly self and deferred to the two older men, especially the one who appeared to be an Amal official. The other man was definitely not an Amal leader, and he didn't look Arabic, either. But he was sure some kind of official. Maybe International Red Cross, I hoped. An ambassador or something?

He was sharp-looking, tall, about forty-five, and close-shaven. He was dressed in light khaki pants, a woven belt, and a cream-colored polo shirt with a country-club logo on it. He had some packs of Marlboros in his left hand. Was he the Marlboro Man from the billboards? He sure looked like him.

He reached out to shake our hands.

119

"Hi, fellows. I am Allyn Conwell, fellow hostage. How are you faring here?"

He introduced us to his escort, a much shorter man named Ali Hamdan, who was the Amal's public relations man. Ali spoke nearly perfect English. Ali was a polite guy who would look into your eyes as you talked to him, all the while keeping his hands behind his back, tightly clasped, and rocking back and forth from heel to toe. An intense sort, small in stature, but strong in mind and position with the Amal.

Both he and Allyn had professional-sounding voices, like radio announcers, and I think they liked listening to each other talk. Allyn seemed an intelligent man who had just accepted a tremendous burden. He was serious and confident in his conversation with us.

"As the leader of the largest hostage group," he explained, "I was asked by the Amal to attend a news conference this evening and say that we are all in good health and are being treated well. I refused to do that unless I was taken around to actually see and talk with everyone. They thought about it awhile and then agreed, so here I am."

We told Allyn we were generally well treated but felt our lives were threatened too often for comfort.

My back was improving, and Stuart's dysentery had let up a bit. So, as hostage conditions go, life wasn't too bad. We were still alive.

Allyn opened a notebook and added our names to a list of thirty-four—a total of thirty-nine hostages, being held in five separate groups.

"I'm going to read off all the names at the press conference tonight," Allyn said.

Somehow, it felt good to be on that list; it made us feel less like military POWs.

Stuart had noticed Jeff Ingalls's name in Allyn's notebook and asked where he was being held. Jeff was a member of the navy dive team, but happened to be carrying a civilian passport, and to our knowledge he had not been identified as military.

Allyn said he was one of a group of four who had been singled out as having "Jewish-sounding names." They were being held by the Hizbollah in a cell two stories underground, but appeared to be safe and in good health.

Allyn told us he wanted a representative from each of the five hostage groups to appear with him at the news conference. A short statement from each group would be read. He asked if we had selected a group leader. Stuart pointed to me.

"Ali, what time will we be back to pick up Mr. Carlson for the conference tonight?" Allyn asked. Ali, in true public relations man fashion, dodged the question.

"Well, this group is farther away in Beirut from the others, and there could be difficulty in sending a car for him," Ali said.

"Perhaps, then, we could take Mr. Carlson back with us, so you will not have to make a special trip later," Allyn replied. You could see the two of them enjoyed verbal jousting and one-upmanship.

"No, that is not necessary. We will send a car at 5:00 P.M., if it is at all possible."

Conwell discussed his role as our spokesman. "I am not going to say anything political, because it could get us in trouble," he said. "We must be concerned with removing all of us from this place."

We agreed that seemed to be a good strategy: come off as reasonable people who can understand the Amal's position while not necessarily agreeing or disagreeing. Just some confused tourists caught in the crossfire of a muddy geopolitical clash. All we want is to go home.

"I have told the Amal I will not allow them to write anything for me to say. I will make my own statements, based on my observations and discussions with all the hostage groups," Conwell said.

That sounded fair to us.

Of course, no one came to pick me up later. I don't think they wanted a military man at the news conference, for fear he would tell the truth—that we were being held in a jail cell right in the crossfire of the local war and were in serious danger. One military man had been murdered, and I had been beaten mercilessly. They had taken pains to isolate us here, not among the general populace, but in the house of the Amal military commander.

Then, too, they remembered the fire power of the USS *New Jersey*, the World War II battleship parked just down the block. When that ship let loose a couple of years before, it terrorized the Shia neighborhoods. The navy said it was looking for the PLO—it sure found a lot of Shi'ites, our guards had told us.

We wondered how Allyn would fare against the international

press vultures. As it happened, the media were too much for the Amal's first attempt at a news conference; we heard the chaos via BBC. The Amal weren't expecting 300 reporters in full battle gear, cameras at the ready.

The BBC reported that one French newsman got too close to the hostages, and a burly militiaman picked him up by the hair and carried him out of the room. We heard that militiamen smashed some cameras and beat up some reporters. But the news media also provided a mob action, yelling and screaming questions to the five hostages at the front table and surging in like an electronic tidal wave.

The Amal leaders beat a hasty retreat to regroup. When it started again, the media were better behaved. A few head bashings had evidently cooled their zeal a little.

Conwell took the lead role, as he'd discussed with us. He was mildly critical of President Reagan, saying he wished more was being done by the administration to secure our freedom. He urged the president not to send in a SWAT team or the Delta Force to rescue us, because such a mission "will only cause, in our estimation, additional unneeded and unwanted deaths among innocent people."

Conwell said we were now in the hands of more reasonable people than the original hijackers, which, for the most part, was true. Anyone would have been more reasonable than Crazy and Hitler.

Conwell said we all feared for our safety, though, and were worried about the emotional stress the crisis was having on our families back home.

He ended with a diplomatic statement designed to pacify just about everyone from Khomeini to Reagan and all Lebanese militias in between.

"Our basic position again is simply this: regardless of who has done wrong prior to today, and several people have done wrong, whole countries have made errors; we make no condemnations, we condone nothing. We simply say if any country is holding people illegally, be it Lebanon here or be it Israel there, or be it America across the seas, let's let innocent and free peoples go home. If a person is not a legitimate prisoner of war or a prisoner due to other crimes, let's all use common sense. Let's let honesty and faith in your fellow man prevail and get innocent people where they belong—with their loved ones."

Good show, we thought.

The only problem was, my group and the four held by the Hizbollah were in dangerous straits, and we wished Allyn had stressed more strongly the need for urgency in the negotiations and that he hadn't altogether discouraged the use of force to rescue us.

Our thoughts were on the American Embassy hostages in Iran, who languished more than a year in the hands of fanatical Shi'ites.

16
Looney Tunes

We had been on edge for what seemed an eternity, with Looney Tune interludes between terror-filled segments of "The Twilight Zone." Sometimes we could laugh at the antics of our guards, but the chuckles were often followed by more tension, fear, and uncertainty.

Ali and his ever-suspicious, chain-smoking chaplain, the Disciple, found a navy manual in Bob Stetham's duffle bag, which had been left in the guards' room.

"This book say you make war!" the Disciple accused, triumph in his eyes as he fired up another Winston.

"No, no, we are construction divers; no combat, no war," Stuart said. "Look at the diagrams—these are construction procedures. The book tells us how to build things under water. No weapons."

For a long time, Ali and the Disciple flipped back and forth through the pages, arguing in Arabic over the illustrations and words. Finally, they left, taking the book with them.

"Good thing that was *Volume One* and not *Volume Two*," said Clint.

"*Volume Two?*" I said.

"Combat procedures," he said.

I blew a breath of relief. This roller-coaster existence was getting to be too much. I began to wonder if Stuart might be right—brainwashing is supposed to be most effective if they can keep you off-balance for hours and hours and hours.

We had awakened Friday morning to an upbeat note. The early news on BBC radio told us the U.S. Sixth Fleet was in position off the coast of Beirut.

We swapped hopeful grins as the newscaster ticked off names of some of the mightiest warships the world has ever known:

- The USS *Nimitz*, the world's second largest nuclear-powered aircraft carrier, bristling with rockets, guided missiles, and a ninety-five aircraft capability.
- The *South Carolina*, a nuclear-powered cruiser packing eighty guided missiles and some big, big guns.
- The *Kidd*, a powerful destroyer with five-inch guns, an arsenal of SAMs, and torpedoes.
- The *Kalamazoo*, carrying Sea Sparrow missiles and four three-inch guns.
- The *Saipan*, an amphibious assault ship loaded with choppers and a Sea Sparrow missle system.
- The *Nashville*, an amphibious transport dock ship with its own assault choppers and twin three-inch guns.
- The *Spartansburg County*, a tank-landing ship armed with rockets and four three-inch guns.

The British newscaster gave the usual dry delivery, but listening between the lines, we knew that Nabih Berri, demanding that Uncle Sam pull back, was blowing his cork.

Nabih Berri, the great Shia leader with an American green card, was telling the Sixth Fleet to back off twelve kilometers: "Then we will consider releasing the hostages." We knew from BBC's reports that the fleet was already twelve kilometers offshore. But who had a yardstick? That Berri's a smart politician, we said. He can stop the U.S. Navy while it is still at anchor. Impressive.

It both worried and reassured us knowing the Sixth Fleet was poised—for whatever.

"If they try a rescue," I said, "we could end up shot before anyone could get to us. We've got to be ready to run for it."

We couldn't be certain, but we thought U.S. Military Intelligence should have our location pinpointed since the Amal had made no effort to keep us out of sight from passersby. But we had no idea where the other hostage groups were being held and suspected that also could pose critical logistical problems for any rescue forces.

"Most likely, the Sixth Fleet is only there to use as an ace in the hole in the negotiations," I said.

Still, as we whiled away the day at cards, exercises, and occasional showers to cool off in the suffocating heat, we were feeling more confident of our chances.

Late in the afternoon, Hassan and a younger guard we didn't know took us upstairs to the office of Joe's older brother, the Amal militia's combat commander. On the wall was a prominently displayed picture of the commander with the Ayatollah Khomeini. The room had a beautiful Persian rug on the floor and ornate furniture.

Hassan got out some cards, and we all sat down to play cards. I was a little worried, because here we were, five American military men, playing cards, drinking pop, and smoking cigarettes in the office of the Amal commander.

The phone rang twice, and Hassan talked in Arabic. He didn't explain to us what he said, or who was on the line. We decided that it was not wise for us to be in the office, so we persuaded Hassan to move the card game into the adjoining room.

The younger guard was gazing out the window, idly bouncing his M-16 on the floor, muzzle-end down. We were getting nervous, because the gun was set on automatic and anything could . . .

"Whap, whap-whap-whap-whap!"

The gun literally danced across the floor, punching holes through the marble and concrete and sending bullets, chips, and dust flying everywhere. We dived for cover.

Hassan lunged for the gun, caught it, and switched it on safe. If he hadn't managed to grab the gun, it would have sprayed the room and slaughtered everyone.

The young guards were terrified. They'd shot up the room, which now had holes in the floor—and they knew they'd be in big trouble with their elders. They frantically tried to sweep the debris into the holes, then cover them with a big rug.

We were more than scared. We were mad. Clint Suggs decided to act. He got up and took the weapon from Hassan, removed its magazine and put it down on a couch. "Take us back to our basement," Clint demanded.

We went downstairs and slammed the door, locking it behind us. Clint was enraged, but said nothing. He went into the other room and sat down, just staring at the wall.

I entered the room softly.

"Clint, are you okay, man?"

"It's all right. I just need a little time by myself, to cool off. I'll be out in a few minutes."

Meanwhile, the two boys were banging on the door, demanding to be let in. We were all angry at them, and considered ignoring their knocks.

But I told the men, "Look, we need to cooperate with these guys If we have problems with the young guards, we could end up in the hands of the Hizbollah. We'll just have to draw another line if we need to and keep a little distance between us and them."

We let them in. Hassan was distraught. "Please, you must not tell our teacher, or anyone, about the gun going off. We could be punished severely for that. It was an accident, and we did not mean to harm anyone. Please, accept apologies from us."

Yes, we forgive you, we told them.

They left and we locked our door again. I went and talked with Clint again. "Look, we shouldn't tell anyone about this incident, at least for now. We've got something on them, and we may need a favor returned. Anyway, Hassan likes us and they might replace him with a thug."

Clint agreed. Later that afternoon we heard a loud commotion upstairs, with many raised voices. It sounded like Hassan was pleading with his teachers. After that, some of our guards carried sidearms only.

The roller coaster nosedived again at about 10:00 in the evening. Hassan, our best interpreter, wasn't around at the moment that Ali and the Disciple abruptly stalked into our cell.

"You come," Ali said brusquely. The guards with them motioned us toward the door with the barrels of their rifles.

We flipped sharp, questioning looks at each other.

"Where are you taking us?" we asked. Their answer was a look that said, "Move out."

"This may be it, guys," I said, not worrying about whether the guards understood. "If it looks like we're going to be shot, be ready to run."

In silence, the guards herded us into the back of a waiting VW van, which immediately lurched forward and barreled down the narrow street.

In addition to being uptight about what we were in for, we were about to learn something about the rules of the road, Beirut-style. The van had to be hitting at least fifty as it careened down alleys and streets too narrow for comfort. The driver never traveled more than one block in a straight line and was constantly swerving left or right to dodge debris and bomb craters.

Even more startling was their way of warning pedestrians and other traffic to get out of the way at intersections. The driver and the guards would stick their .45s and .38s out the window and cut loose into the air. Apparently, the understanding was that anyone too slow to move would have to dodge the next volley.

This get-the-hell-out-of-the-way-or-else substitute for the American horn toot seemed to be traditional for the Amal. Thereafter, every time we loaded into a van to go somewhere, it was the same thing.

Never again will I complain about the crazy drivers back home, I promised myself over and over again.

After a long time, the van screeched to a halt beside a tall apartment building. The door slid back, and the guards motioned us out of the van. We stepped out warily. Nudging us with their gun barrels, the guards marched us down a long, descending ramp into an underground garage.

The St. Valentine's Day massacre scene, I thought.

We bottomed out on the garage floor. It was pitch-black. I sucked in my breath and tuned my ears for the sounds of gun bolts. The lights flared on.

My eyes focused and zeroed in on piles of suitcases and bags along the wall facing us. It was the luggage from Flight 847.

Trembling with relief, we pawed through the heap to find our gear. The navy divers found their blue dive bags containing their face masks, flipper fins, and wet suits. I came up with only one of my suitcases.

No telling where the other one ended up, I thought, remembering my conversation with Uli when I had gotten aboard Flight 847.

The ride back to our basement cell was even less comfortable since we were now stuffed into the VW van with all our luggage and the suddenly smiling and friendly guards. The driver couldn't seem to keep his eyes on the road. He kept sticking his head out the window every now and then to look closely at some passing object, twisting his neck to get a better look after it had gone by.

The guards pressed close, excited, as we lugged our stuff into the cell. It didn't take much to figure out what they wanted. We popped open our luggage and stepped back, watching them dig in like kids into a cookie jar. They were looking for more military clothing—anything they could wear.

I had only civilian clothing in my suitcase, so I got off without any loss. Hassan came late to the forage and seemed a little disappointed. I gave him a pair of designer jogging shorts to use as a swimsuit. He was so thrilled that he just had to give me something in return, but the only thing he had handy was his militia ID card. He showed it to me with pride. It listed his family tree, dating all the way back to the prophet Mohammed, in both Arabic and English.

He gave me the card, and I had hoped to keep it, but one of his superiors came around later and took it back.

The two Hassans then discovered the divers' wet suits. Wow! They'd never seen anything like that. They pulled and tugged their way into the suits, attached the fins, then waddled around our cell like Lloyd Bridges on a binge.

"Can we go down to the sea and swim under the water?" Hassan asked.

"Well, you can wear the fins, but if you are not familiar with the wet suits, you will probably sink," said Stuart. "Oh," Hassan said, realizing his idea was not so good. He and Hassan II continued clomping around the cell in the fins and wet suits, feigning dives and practicing swim strokes. Finally tiring of the game, they took off the suits and left. We doubled over in laughter.

Hassan arranged a special treat for us the following day, Saturday. It was their Sabbath, and the other guards were away for a few hours. After checking the building to make sure no one was around, Hassan motioned for us to follow him up the stairs.

First, we walked around the apartment being constructed on the third floor for Joe and his wife. We marveled that the Amal could blissfully keep building in the middle of a combat zone. We took our time looking at the carpentry and masonry, but our minds were reaching higher.

"Too bad we can't see the roof," I remarked casually. "I do roofing work at home, you know."

"You want to see? We go," Hassan said, leading the way.

We traded knowing looks—this was our chance to get the lay of the land in case we needed to carry through with our escape plans. We were beginning to believe we might be negotiated out of this, but there was always the threat of a long, long wait.

Trying not to be obvious, we kept Hassan busy pointing out this and that, all the while memorizing as much detail as we could, our eyes searching the horizons as well as the surrounding neighborhood, picking our route to the sea.

Although we had ulterior motives, we couldn't help marveling at the stubborn beauty of this war-shattered city. Through a blue haze, we could see mountains rising all around us, with beautiful high-rises and office buildings climbing right up the sides. To the north lay Beirut, a sprawling mass of tall buildings and short, and to the east the coastline of the magnificent Mediterranean. Only a block to the west was the airport, surrounded by bomb-shattered buildings, debris, and burned-out cars.

The most beautiful sight of all loomed in the background—the *Nimitz*, appearing huge even in the distance, and the ships of the Sixth Fleet.

We came up with enough detail to plot a course to the water, figuring we could swim out a couple of hundred yards, then cut up the shoreline to where a lot of boats were anchored near some hotels. A boat could take us out to the Sixth Fleet before our captors knew we were gone.

From that rooftop, we could see the hijacked jetliner, where the pilot and copilot were still being held by the hijackers. We also made note of the Amal checkpoints. Our building was near the edge of Amal territory, which would make it easier for us to make it to the highway.

I suppose we could have overpowered Hassan and gotten away right then. I doubt that Hassan would have tried to stop us. He liked us too much to shoot us. But we knew our escape might endanger the other hostages. No, better to give the negotiations a full chance before making our move.

We filed the information away in our minds and settled on a waiting game.

Those were our worst days because we were locked up in our cell for long hours. It was awfully hot down there.

My routine was to awaken at about 7:00 A.M., take a shower, and wash out my underwear in the old washtub. Stuart followed me, then the others. We spent a lot of time exercising and sunning ourselves under the back window, which let in sunlight until about 9:30 A.M. My bruised muscles were healing, and I was beginning to do isometrics and to limber up by walking in circles with Stuart.

We listened to BBC and played cards while our laundry dried. We scrubbed up the cell every afternoon, mostly to keep busy.

The dust never seemed to stop drifting in through the window, and we took out some of our frustrations pounding our bedding in the alley between the buildings. I think pounding those foam pads was good therapy.

That little radio given to us by the Amal guards was our only link to the outside world. The BBC was the only station we could understand. The BBC reports were on everything imaginable and excruciatingly detailed—several hours, for example, discussing reforestation of Vietnam.

But, dry though they were, the BBC reports were precise, accurate, and on the mark. It was from the BBC that we learned of the French and Swiss efforts to mediate the hostage crisis and of the maneuverings taking place between the Amal leaders and the U.S. State Department.

The BBC didn't say much, though, about what was happening back home in the States. Upon our return, we were surprised to learn of the outpouring of prayers, yellow ribbons, billboards, and rallies of support all across the U.S. If we had known about that while in our dreary, bug-infested Beirut cell, our spirits would have soared.

On the second Sunday of our Beirut vacation, the BBC broadcast an Anglican church service from London, and we made it our own, praying along with the radio—until the power went off. We broke out the guitar again and joined voices in singing "How Great Thou Art" and some other hymns.

The British church service had focused on the apostle Paul's sufferings in prison, when the Lord had appeared to encourage him, and I was thinking about that as I sat on a pillow near the basement window. Suddenly, a beam of sunlight streamed through the window. The fears I had lived with for days evaporated.

But, later that evening, the roller coaster took another dive. The power came back on, and at 9:00 the BBC took us into the mind of the well-known conservative American commentator, George Will.

Until now, I had always liked George's way of thinking. He's an Illinois boy, too, from Champaign. But the BBC said George had said the United States should take a tough stand against international terrorism. That we agreed with.

But, the BBC report droned on, Mr. Will, who spoke for the conservative right—which is my end of the political spectrum— was saying the U.S. should be prepared to take some losses in standing firm against terrorists.

Since U.S. nuclear policy involves trade-offs, the report went on, Will reasoned that U.S. terrorism policy should accept trade-offs, too. He saw no reason why the U.S. shouldn't be willing to trade the lives of the thirty-nine hostages for the principle of a hard-line stand against terrorism.

The navy divers were shaken to the core.

"More sword rattling," I tried to tell them, not really convinced myself.

17
The Red Cross Meeting

On Tuesday, June 25, we were playing blackjack with our by-now-dog-eared playing cards when Ali and the Winston-smoking Amal we called "Disciple" stalked into our room.

Disciple always made us feel uneasy. He apparently prided himself greatly on his knowledge, and although not much older than the militiamen, he was constantly lecturing them on the rights and wrongs of the earth, according to the teachings of the Koran.

He was especially down on Clint. Hassan had told us that Disciple taught them that black people were horribly oppressed in America. With Clint obviously our equal, some of the guards were asking questions they hadn't asked before. Clint gave Hassan a copy of Kareem Abdul-Jabbar's book, which not only seemed to contradict the rampant oppression Disciple preached, but it even had a picture of Jabbar, a practicing Muslim achieving wondrous feats on the basketball court. Other pictures showed Jabbar in his spacious mansion and driving luxury cars.

Disciple had been furious at Clint for giving Hassan the book.

Apparently the chaplain had now decided to change his approach. He and Ali motioned for us to join them, sitting in a circle by the window and—Would you believe it?—began singing to us in Arabic.

We couldn't understand the words but figured they were religious hymns. Apparently there were happy thoughts in the lyrics, because they would smile for effect. We could do nothing but listen politely, although it was interesting. Stuart, who never let up in the pursuit of detail that might be of value in a military situation, listened for patterns. In one long song, he counted twenty-four verses, for what it was worth.

The concert ended, they left, and all we could do was look at each other blankly and shrug. We were hungry and scrounged for something to eat. All we found was some three-day-old pita bread and two-day-old sour cream. I think that's what touched off my subsequent bout with dysentery.

Hassan had the day off, and when young Pistol came on duty, we told him we were awfully hungry. Concern flashed through his sad eyes, and he left. Sometime later, our number two Hassan came to the door and said, "Come, friends, we go have dinner with Pistol."

We loaded into the VW van, and Hassan II drove about two blocks down the street to—of all things—an outdoor cafe. He motioned for us to wait and went inside, leaving us sitting there alone in the van. We could have driven away, but we had passed through checkpoints on the way, and this wasn't familiar terrain.

Hassan II returned in a few minutes. "Pistol not here, but no worry," he said, shifting the van into gear.

After a few more blocks, he pulled up in front of the Beirut version of the Colonel and McBurger King, all rolled into one. It had a big red chicken on the sign. Pistol came running out as we drove up and, with a big grin, shoved bags of hamburgers, french fries, and Pepsis through the window. Number two Hassan drove away, and we dug in, devouring the hamburgers, which were a meal in themselves, loaded with vegetables and sauces, surrounding a tiny piece of ground beef.

"Did Pistol pay for this stuff out of his money?" I asked Hassan. "No, we all broke," he said. "But Pistol got good credit!"

Hassan kept driving as we chowed down. I suddenly realized he didn't seem to be heading back toward our basement cell.

Something's up, I thought, studying Hassan's face in the rearview mirror. He looked pleased with himself, but maybe it was because he and Pistol had succeeded in doing us a big favor with the food.

It was about eight o'clock in the evening when we stopped at a walled schoolyard. A lot of militiamen with automatic weapons were standing around.

We were led through a door in the wall, emerging into the yard, which had a three-story yellow school building in the center. The playground had a basketball hoop at one end and concrete benches around the perimeter. About forty school desks were lined up in rows in the center of the playground. The courtyard was filled with people: our fellow hostages from Flight 847. Were we all going home?

Vicente Garza, the Spanish-American hostage from Laredo, Texas, recognized me and rushed up to put his arms around me. "We have all been worried about you," he said. "We knew you were badly beaten, but no one would tell us if you were . . ."

"Yes, I'm alive, I'm alive, and feeling better," I smiled. "I'm a little stiff and sore, but alive.

"Have you got a cigarette?" I asked Garza.

"Here," he said as he handed me one. "Don't they give you cigarettes?"

"Yes, our guards share everything they have, including food, but they don't have much," I replied. "Vicente, why have they brought us all here?"

"The International Red Cross is supposed to meet with us," he said.

"Well, that may be one step closer to getting out of here," I said. He nodded.

The divers found their buddy, Jeff Ingalls, who had only temporarily eluded identification as military.

Ingalls, being held by the Hizbollah, said his guard treated him the same as the civilians in his group.

"That's a good sign," I said. "It means the fact that we're military may not be as bad as we feared. They may be getting to know us as people."

We asked Jeff about his group's treatment by the Hizbollah. He assured us they were not being mistreated, but it was virtual prison confinement in a dark cell. They had no communication at all with their guards, except for the one who brought their food. They had rats.

Then Ingalls said his group's only visitor had been one of the hijackers from the airplane, confirming our suspicions that the Hizbollah had carried out the whole incident. "He walked in one day and asked if we recognized him," Ingalls said. "When we didn't answer, he pulled out his pearl-handled .45 and showed it to us." Now they knew for sure who it was, and so did I when he described him: it was the one I called "Hitler."

Luckily, Hitler's visit was just a social call.

I talked with several other hostages and discovered the truth of that old saying, "It's a small world."

The two Catholic priests from suburban Chicago weren't really strangers. Father Jim McLoughlin had pastored a church in Rockford, and Father Tom Dempsey had known one of the supervisors in my roofing company.

The hostages idled away some of the time playing volleyball or walking around. Clint batted the volleyball back and forth with some of the Amal guards.

Suddenly, the steel gate swung open, and a militiaman buzzed through on an old Harley Davidson motorcycle. He roared around and around the open space in the playground, popping wheelies and showing off, finally stopping and asking if anyone wanted a ride. Blake Synnestvedt, a young hostage from Pennsylvania, took the cycle for a spin and popped some wheelies himself.

The militiaman took over again and, with Blake on the back, roared out through the gate and took him on a hell-bent-for-anywhere tour of the neighborhood, I guess.

The Red Cross showed up at about nine o'clock—two young Swiss, dressed in black leather jackets, black pants, short-sleeved shirts, and narrow, black ties. One man was tall and thin; he headed the Red Cross in Beirut. The second, a man in his mid-twenties, was a doctor. They had us all sit down at the school desks, forming in five groups according to how we were being held. We were to fill out forms listing our names and family contacts. If we had a serious health problem, the doctor would check us out. The sketchy information would be relayed to our families in the States.

"That's all we can do," the Red Cross leader said. "We can send no messages for you unless it involves a life-and-death situation."

One of the hostages, a middle-aged man, became quite insistent. He wanted to send a message to his business partner to have new keys made for his car, his office, his house, and his desk. The Red Cross man said that would be impossible, but the hostage insisted his business would be in serious trouble if the keys he had lost in the hijacking were not replaced. I felt sorry for the man. He seemed to be cracking under the stress. Father Dempsey began talking softly with the man to calm him.

Allyn Conwell, who had been speaking unofficially for all of us, said he was uncomfortable in assuming that authority and suggested the hostages should formally elect a leader to speak for all the groups. After some discussion we all agreed that Captain Testrake, who was still on the airplane, should be our leader once he rejoined us, but that until then Allyn would act in his place.

Allyn then asked Ali Hamdan, the Amal's top spokesman, for an update on the negotiations.

"I am sorry to say, it doesn't look too good," Ali said, hands clasped behind him and rocking back and forth, as he had done when we first met him with Conwell in our basement cell.

He said President Reagan was threatening force, a takeover of the Beirut airport, and a blockade of the harbor, and—

"We didn't want to hear the bad news," Allyn cut in, still jousting verbally with Ali, as he'd done before.

"We want the good news," Allyn continued. "We all know a lot of this is sword-rattling. The Israelis have just released 31 Shi'ite prisoners and have indicated they will be setting the other 735 free. We will be going home very soon."

He gave Ali a sly, Texas trader smile as he said it.

As we filed out of the schoolyard to return to our groups, the Swiss doctor embraced Dr. Richard Moon, one of the hostages, and gave him his medical bag and stethoscope. We loaded back into the VW van, and number two Hassan drove us back to our cell—only this time he took the direct route up the four-lane, by the airport. It was then we realized the building where we were being held was the first checkpoint into Shi'ite territory. We could simply walk away without worrying about getting mowed down by machine guns.

"It's looking up, guys," I said, once we were back in our room.

And then all hell broke loose.

It started with an artillery barrage. We could hear the rounds whistling over the roof of our building, crashing and exploding on the mountainside to the south.

"They must be into it with the Druse," Stuart said. Or it could be the Palestinians, I thought, or the Israelis, or the USS *New Jersey*. It was loud, whoever was dishing it out.

Suddenly gunfire erupted in the street just outside. We doused the light, clamped the window shut, put out our cigarettes, and lay quietly along the wall. Small arms fire and machine guns rattled the air. One grenade exploded so close we could hear the shrapnel splattering the outdoor walls of our building. It kept up until about 3:00 A.M., then stopped abruptly.

That was the rule in this crazy city. No matter how fierce the battle, from 3:00 A.M. to noon everyone takes a break.

At about 10:00 Wednesday morning, Hassan number one took us outside for some air. A section of the low wall where we had sat to play the guitar and sing songs was gone.

"What happened to the wall?" I asked Hassan.

He shrugged. "Boom-boom, pfft."

We had decided we shouldn't ask too many questions about what the sudden fight was all about. Our hosts didn't like questions.

Clint and Ken broke out a jump rope and began skipping exercises in the narrow alley. Hassan had to show them he, too, could skip rope. That led to a demonstration of "Ranger" tactics.

"Watch," said Hassan, showing off. He began a scissors walk up between the narrow, three-foot gap between the walls.

He was about twenty feet up when we noticed the wall of our building seemed to be unstable. It started leaning outward.

"Aayiiii," Hassan hissed from above. We rushed around the opposite side and pushed against the wall, as Hassan scampered down to safety.

One more heavy mortar attack, I thought, and the walls of the building would collapse. We would have to escape soon or risk being buried alive.

Later that day, Joe's older brother, the military commander, came by to ask how we were faring.

"I understand you showed some of our people how to work an M-16," he said casually—too casually, I thought.

Ken had demonstrated an M-16 strip-down for one of the Amal militiamen.

"It's made the same way as rifles we used in basic training; only we didn't use combat weapons; it was one that used a small .22 cartridge," Stuart said. Again we were on edge, for fear we were being singled out as combat soldiers.

That concern grew, as early in the evening Ali came back with an Amal patrol—eight men—lugging an M-60 machine gun. "Show us how to fire this," he said. "Tear it down for us."

We aren't familiar with that weapon, we said. They left disappointed.

"That is the gun I'm trained on," Ken said.

"They're suspicious; they're setting us up," Stuart said.

"I don't think so," I told him. "It seems to me that they've scrounged weapons from wherever they can get them and don't know how to work or maintain them. I think they were looking for some weapons training. But we won't cooperate."

They don't need our help in figuring out how to kill each other, I thought.

For the next few days, things got rough. For some reason, we stopped getting our regular meal deliveries. Much of our food had consisted of airline meals, delivered daily from Middle East Airlines. But for nearly four days, the deliveryman didn't come at all.

Had something gone wrong? Were the Amal taking a new, tougher line? We didn't know. We just got hungry, that's all, surviving on some bread and cheese we got from our guards, and water. Before we turned out the lights, Joe came by to see us. We told him very politely that we were hungry. He was not surprised. He said there was a new delivery boy, and evidently he didn't know this house was on the hostage meals-on-wheels route.

Joe apologized. He would fix things.

During our second week, we saw Beirut almost as if we were visitors from another planet. When we were outside the Amal house, we observed the everyday street scenes of West Beirut. What we visitors learned was that we were looking at ourselves— through a distorted funhouse mirror. In a sense, popular culture of the United States created these people. We gave them the Marlboro Man, and, as we saw, he is more popular than the Ayatollah Man.

Beirut television is a clue. Our guards occasionally allowed us to watch their banged-up, portable black and white, which gave us insight into the city's twisted personality.

The reception, of course, was terrible, so I asked Hassan for some wire to rig up an antenna. He promptly ripped down 20 feet of electrical wire from the passageway and brought it to me—with four light blubs still attached. I hooked it to the TV set with the bulbs in place and tied the other end to the bars of the cell door. Then we got beautiful reception.

We were treated to a steady barrage of American television programs, American-style commercials, and unabashedly uncensored news reports.

"Yahoo! Bang-bang!" said an excited Hassan one night, as the familiar faces from our youth, the "Bonanza" regulars, came charging across our Beirut screen. Hoss Cartwright talking Arabic can be a cultural shock. But it's no wonder "Bonanza" is a popular show in Beirut. The Wild West probably lives nowhere else but.

"Magnum P.I." is a big hit, and "Dallas's" J.R. is something of a factional chieftan in the Beirut tradition, controlling real estate and petrodollars, albeit without tanks and howitzers.

Commercials featured loud rock and roll music, with macho guys and sexy girls in designer jeans, sipping Pepsi down on the beach or while driving around in a Mercedes Benz convertible.

We watched a Clark Gable movie with Arabic subtitles. We heard the news in French and English.

Another show we enjoyed was a Lebanese version of "Star Search," complete with an applause meter and a panel of judges. First some homespun rock and roll, followed by a polka band. The audience loved that. They clapped in time with the music and danced in the aisles. Then we heard some Lebanese folk songs, done up in classic style by a band of generic militia men, complete with ammunition belts and AK-47s.

"That group's going to win," I told my fellow viewers. "They've got the guns."

Sure enough, the judges voted them the top group on the show. Smart judges. Alive judges.

The TV set taught us that Beirutis are westernized beyond imagination. The women wear high-heeled sandals, tight designer jeans, silk blouses, and makeup. No chadors in evidence. The men also wear designer jeans with neatly pressed short-sleeved shirts, They almost all sport cowboy belts with big brass buckles.

Late Wednesday night, our guards brought a video recorder into our cell and we hooked it to the television set. They had tapes of three Al Pacino flicks, including *Dog Day Afternoon*. To top off the canine theme, the movie *Hot Dog* was also included in the VHS library we received. Alas. The machine wasn't as good as the one upstairs and, just like nearly everything else in the building, didn't work properly.

Oh, we had enough electricity, even though the juice comes and goes in modern-day Beirut; our Amal landlords just ran a line up to the electric pole, and tapped into the system. They were very casual about the hookups, too. They just pushed wires into the walls.

I wondered why the place hadn't blown itself up. I don't think the city's electrical inspectors dared challenge their connections—unless the Beirut electrical inspectors carry guns, too, which is a distinct possibility.

After several hours of trying in vain to fix the VCR, we decided it was no use. We hooked up some wire to our steel door, which would act as an antenna. We settled down to "Dallas" instead of Al Pacino.

We loved the diversion, but the gurgling cauldron that is Beirut kept us constantly on guard while in our jail cell.

Despite a decade of civil war, Beirut was still, in 1985, a wide-open city. Because there was no effective government, drug traffic flourished. Smuggling flourished. Free trade flourished, because nobody bothered to collect duties. Beirut is the center of world intrigue. You can buy or sell anything, anyone, any idea. It is at once communistic, anarchistic, capitalistic, socialistic—as I said, wide open.

Beirutis are good bargainers, and they're street-smart. They realize that justice is a by-product of "clout." It's just that they have this bad habit of enforcing the bargains with howitzers. They're dealing, and they'll let you know it.

18
The Carlson Commandos

It was Wednesday, June 26. The concert in Nassau Coliseum went well for Cheap Trick. The band's fifty-minute set, with one encore, got thunderous applause. The fans still loved Cheap Trick, even if the group was warming them up for REO Speedwagon.

Not many of the clapping, foot-stomping, cheering fans realized that Bun E. Carlos wasn't quite up to his usual jackhammer drumming. Oh, he didn't miss any cues or blow any licks; he was just somewhere else.

Kevin Cronin, lead singer for REO Speedwagon, was sensitive to his fellow rocker's burden. He had taken to reminding crowds along the concert tour that Bun's brother was one of the hostages being held—it seemed like a long time now—in Beirut. The first time Kevin had done that, he actually asked the fans to take a moment and pray to God, if they were into that, for Bun's brother. The stage managers weren't expecting it and almost went berserk, fearful that Cronin was taking the hyped-up crowd into a downer.

Backstage, tears rolled down Bun's cheeks as Cronin picked up his acoustic guitar and began strumming chords. The crowd fell silent, mesmerized, it seemed, as Cronin drove the guitar harder and harder into an expression of wailing emotion, a completely unrehearsed lead-in to REO's hit, "Riding the Storm Out."

Bun called home right after the concert. "Tell Mom we just had 14,000 rock fans praying for Kurt," he told his wife, Ellen.

Mark, Kris, and the kids were waiting for Bun down in the basement dressing room. They laughed a bit about how Kris had been furious at Mark the first time they discussed the "mission."

"Mark called me from the hospital and said he had some good news, but it was crazy, and he couldn't talk about it," Kris said. "I asked him if someone was in the room that he didn't want to talk in front of, and he said, no, he was all alone, but he couldn't talk about it anyway.

"I said, 'Mark Carlson, you call me up and tell me you've got some important news, which you are not going to tell me, and there's nobody there listening, but you're still not going to tell me?' He said, 'That's right, I can't tell you.' Well, I said, 'If that's the case, you just don't even bother to come home.'

"Then he comes rushing into the house, won't say a word, just heads out to the backyard, and I'm yelling, 'Mark, what's got into you?' I follow him out into the yard, and then he tells me the telephones and maybe even the house is bugged by the FBI, and we're talking to some people that may be able to get Kurt out of there."

Mark had been filled in by his parents, Ed and Vie, back in Rockford, calling from a pay telephone.

His mother related how she had gotten "the strangest telephone call" on Monday, June 17, before the media descended upon the Carlson household.

"Yes, of course, I remember you," she had told the man on the other end of the line. She was surprised, however, that he remembered her, since they had met only once, briefly, at a social function far from Rockford.

She was aware that the man was powerful and wealthy and recalled that he had some sort of relationship with foreign governments. But why was he calling now?

"We have received your request, but it has not come through the usual channels," the man said.

Vie wanted to say, "What request?" but something told her to wait.

"I just wanted you to know that we are looking into it, and we will be doing all we can to help your son," the man continued.

"Thank you," Vie replied. "I'm sure everything will be all right." She was growing cautious now. Kurt's identity as a hostage still was not supposed to be known to the outside world. What was this man talking about? She was afraid to ask.

"I will get back to you as soon as we have more information," he said.

Vie hung up. She told Ed about the call. Ed was also familiar with the source.

"I don't know what it means," he said. "Maybe . . . well, I just don't know."

Later, at Kurt's office, where Ed took refuge from the news media and kept his son's business going, there had been another call.

Ed now understood. Bun's mysterious telephone call from the concert hall in Buffalo, New York, when he first learned Kurt was a hostage, had set in motion a bizarre chain of events. It also became clear that discretion was of the utmost importance. If the man now offering his assistance should ever be publicly identified, the repercussions could be devastating.

"Our main worry right now is that we don't know if he is badly hurt," Ed said.

"Our people saw him taken off the airplane. He walked to the truck under his own power and appeared to be coherent," the voice said.

"Your people were close enough to see him taken off the plane?" Ed said, astonished.

"I will call you back in exactly six hours," the voice continued. "We will have more information at that time."

Ed noted and logged the time of the next call: exactly five hours and fifty-seven minutes after the first. The message was cryptic but clear.

To himself, he jotted the note:

"Kurt OK, watching TV."

"Wait," Ed said. "How can you be so sure? Do you know that your people have actually seen him?"

"I can assure you this was a visual inspection," the voice said.

Ed had to marvel at this. The entire U.S. government, with all its intelligence-gathering resources, seemed to know little about his son's situation, but this man, an American, had somehow arranged for someone in Beirut to see Kurt in person. Incredible.

There had been other discussions, which Mark, Kris, and Bun were now to hear explained.

The well-dressed man who joined them in the dressing room was indeed impressive. Briefly, he explained that there are thousands of Americans with ties to Lebanon, both Christians and Muslims, and despite the factionalism in Beirut, family ties remain very strong. One group may be at war with another, but, he shrugged, there are ways . . .

He cautioned them again to be wary of discussing this, especially by telephone. "It is our understanding that the FBI or U.S. military intelligence may have your telephones tapped," he said.

"If we are to discuss this matter by telephone, we will speak in terms of an automobile purchase. Our contacts in Beirut have suggested the code name '47 Cadillac.' "

"Have they seen him, these people you've got?" Mark demanded.

The man smiled patiently. "Our contacts have made a visual inspection. He is in excellent condition."

"You're certain of this," Mark persisted. His temper had grown short trying to get information from the United States State Department, and he was still uncertain as to his brother's injuries.

"You are certainly correct in your caution," the man said. "But you must remember, we are dealing with no government officials in this. For all practical purposes, there is no government in Lebanon. Our people must do things in their own way. I cannot share with you exactly how it was done, but I assure you our people have seen him and know that he is well."

"So, what's the gig? How do we get him out?" Bun asked.

"We have people standing by with vehicles and weapons," the man said. "They are prepared to storm the house where your brother is being held and take him out by force if that becomes necessary."

"Great," Bun said. "That's the best damned news I've heard all week. If Reagan screws up, we go get him with our own commandos. It's crazy, but it just might work."

Mark looked worried. His cautious, analytical mind focused on the odds. We're talking bullets here, he thought. People could get killed. Kurt, too, could be caught in the crossfire and killed. It sounded too risky.

"Isn't there some other way?" he asked. "If some innocent person got hurt or killed, Kurt would never forgive himself or us."

"That is understood," the man said. "Your parents and your brother's wife have told us that force should be our last resort— only if it appears there is no hope of gaining his release in other ways.

"Our first option is to try to arrange for his release through a meeting in Beirut between your father and Dr. Berri. It could be arranged so that his release appeared to be a goodwill gesture. The Amal would bring Kurt to Dr. Berri's home to meet your father. Meanwhile, some of the Amal prisoners being held by another faction in Beirut would be released. No one would know that it is actually an exchange of prisoners."

"So, what are we talking here—ransom? How much do we have to raise?" Mark asked. Whatever it took, he felt, the Carlson family could raise the money, but the idea grated. He knew Kurt would not feel good about being bought out if others were left behind.

An impatient look flashed across the man's face. Money had long since ceased to be of importance to him.

"We do this for you because we, too, know the meaning of family love," he said. "Our mutual friends have told us of the remarkable closeness of your family, and we do this for you in that spirit."

Mutual friends? Mark's eyebrows raised. There was more to this than what he had been told. Bun didn't look surprised.

"Of course," the man continued, "we hope that you will repay our kindness with a small favor."

"Here it comes," Bun muttered. His years on the rock and roll circuit had taught him to tread softly among small favors.

"Should we be successful in this," the man said, "perhaps your people could use their influences and expertise to help one of our young musicians become well known in the United States."

"Holy Jesus," Bun said, shaking his head. "This gets crazier by the minute. All we gotta do is pump a Lebanese rock star, and you'll send in commandos to rescue Kurt. Weird."

"This is the family way, is it not?" the man asked.

"That is, indeed, the family way," said Bun.

The rock and roll drummer felt a tremendous sense of relief as he hugged his doctor brother, his sister-in-law, and the kids. Mark and Kris were still uneasy as they drove home. Kris, in particular, had doubts.

"They're calling him a '47 Cadillac because of his birth date," she told Mark. "But Kurt was born in 1946. They could have read his age in the newspapers."

"Maybe they just subtracted wrong," Mark said. But he, too, felt uneasy.

He called his father. "Kurt wouldn't like any of this," he said.

"I know," Ed said. "I've discussed it with your mother and Cheri. My feeling is that Kurt would not want to be saved at the expense of anyone else. It's like the thing about the captain going down with his ship.

"The other thing is, if a bunch of strange people with guns broke in and Kurt didn't know they were trying to rescue him, he just might grab a gun and fight them off."

The New York Times headlines the next day were optimistic. Nabih Berri was saying he felt certain the hostages would soon be free; France was volunteering to take the hostages under its wing; the U.S. government seemed to be strangely silent.

A news blackout, Mark thought. They're talking behind the scenes. Thank God.

The Carlson Commandos would not be unleashed.

19
The Banquet

Something was up. It was Thursday afternoon, June 27. Hassan came down to see us.

"I want to give you my address," he told me. I borrowed a piece of paper from Stuart's notebook and gave it to Hassan. He wrote "Beirut, Lebanon. Hassan Zayoun, Almamora Street, Building Fahre, Number 1."

"Please, can you send me a visa? I want to come to America and work."

We had talked before about my business and how I was building office buildings in Rockford. Hassan wanted to be a carpenter. He could construct good windows and doors, he said.

"Ha," said Clint. "You should fix up this dump before you try your luck in the States." Clint pointed to the crumbling walls and window frames.

Hassan was offended. "I have done much work in this building. You should have seen it before. It was worse."

One by one, other guards appeared, each giving us addresses and asking for sponsorship to come to the U.S.

Three of them—the two Hassans and young Pistol—had become

especially close to us. I don't think they had a bad bone in their bodies. They wanted to go back to school, where they had played soccer with other kids who they were now supposed to be fighting, because those kids were Palestinians and they were Shi'ites.

Then Hassan Zayoun pointed at a *Time* magazine we had been reading. He picked it up and leafed through it until he found a picture.

Both Hassans put the magazine to their lips and kissed the picture. It was of Allyn Conwell. "He is a good man," they both said.

Well, Conwell pulled it off, I thought. He succeeded in gaining the Amal's confidence by forcing them to think of us as separate from the American government. They may have hated President Reagan, but they sure trusted Allyn. Maybe that trust would help us.

Around dinner time, the delivery boy finally showed up with all kinds of food and cigarettes. For me, he was a few days too late. I was coming down with a bad case of dysentery, probably from eating spoiled leftovers.

We invited the guards in for dinner and talked about going home. The negotiations were still secret, but for the first time the BBC news commentaries sounded optimistic. With a full stomach and a dream of going home, I slept like a baby.

On Friday morning, we ate breakfast with Hassan and Pistol outside in the passageway. We watched "Laurel and Hardy" on the guards' TV. Huddled around the television, Hassan and Pistol looked more like kids than guards.

At about 3:00 in the afternoon, Ali stalked in with four tough-looking guards wearing green arm bands. I wondered if they were the Amal version of the Secret Service.

"Hurry up and be quiet," Ali instructed gruffly, motioning for us to gather our gear.

We hustled but took time to clean up the room. We were feeling a little cocky now that we thought we were about to be released, and one way we had of showing it was to make sure we left our cell cleaner than we had found it.

The navy divers even carefully rolled up the old tattered foam pads we had been sleeping on. Ali looked impatient and told us again to hurry. We wasted no more time getting out of there. Hassan and Pistol were not around to say good-bye.

We knew from the BBC that the Syrians had gotten involved in the negotiations for our release. The hostage crisis was making them look bad, because the Amal are considered Syria's allies. Also, Syria does not want to encourage the fundamentalist Shi'ites like the Hizbollah, for fear their fanaticism will spread across the border to Syria, a secular Muslim state.

The four militiamen with green arm bands loaded us into another VW ambulance. They drove us by two camouflaged howitzers at the bottom of the street; we also saw a Russian-built tank. They took us down a broad, once beautiful boulevard, with ocean on one side and luxury high rises on the other. Many of the buildings were damaged, whole chunks of them blown away. It was as if there had been a war along Lake Shore Drive or Miami Beach Boulevard. The guards said some of the buildings had been hit by Israeli fire, some by the U.S. Navy, but most by factional Muslim and Christian Lebanese fighting. Most of the luxury hotels had been blown away, but down on the beaches, Lebanese still sunbathed, frolicked in the surf, and behaved as if things were normal. Come to think of it, after ten years of civil war, things probably *were* normal. I thought of the guard Pistol, who, at age twelve, cannot remember a time when rockets didn't sail overhead, when tanks didn't rumble down the street, when going to a soccer game didn't mean crossing ten military checkpoints on the way.

We passed by the Amal's basic training camp and several howitzer positions before rolling to a stop at a four-story apartment building. We were taken upstairs. My eyes popped when I saw the guard standing in front of the apartment door. He was huge, about 300 pounds, and he wore a T-shirt that said "Eat the Rich."

The door opened, and I was pleasantly surprised to see another group of Americans. Dr. Moon from North Carolina greeted us and introduced us to his eight-hostage crew. They had been kept in a vacant apartment with two bedrooms, a bathroom with tub and shower, living room, and dining room. We all shook hands, and Dr. Moon asked if we were hungry, pointing to a table stacked with

Middle East Airlines meals. We laughed and told them about our food mix-up, suggesting that they'd been receiving our food as well as theirs.

We got the grand tour of the place, hosted by the building's owner. The man's small son, about seven, had come to know the hostages during their stay, Dr. Moon told me. "We taught him to play cards."

Dr. Moon said four of his group had to stay in the basement of the building for a few days, which was not pleasant, because rats were among the visitors. Since the breakdown of civilian government, garbage has not been picked up in Beirut, and heaps of garbage can be found all over.

Apparently the Amal weren't as careful to hide Moon's group as they were us. They were not military people.

"We've met Nabih Berri," one of the group told me, as if to say he'd had an audience with the Pope. Well, in this case, he had.

Berri was a very personable man, he said. "We were very impressed with him."

Besides being the Amal leader, Berri also was minister of justice and minister of South Lebanon in the weak Lebanese government, where the Christian Amin Gemayel, brother of the slain Bashir Gemayel, was president, and the Druse Muslim leader, Walid Jumblatt, was minister of public works. I bet Jumblatt is the only guy with patronage jobs.

"Have you been taken out for dinner?" Dr. Moon asked.

"Not exactly," I replied, remembering the "Red Chicken" carry-out.

"We've been out twice to the Miami Beach Restaurant."

"To the what?"

Moon explained that the Amal had taken his group out to eat one night at about 10:00. They were driving down a once-trendy street in Beirut, now all but reduced to rubble. Amid the devastation was a building pretty much intact, Moon said. In front was a large, neon sign, hanging slightly off center, but blazing away with white, scroll-type neon writing announcing "Miami Beach Restaurant." Palm trees, of course, were painted around the writing.

"It was late, and the restaurant was closed. But the owners are

Amal sympathizers, and they live upstairs. So they opened it up for us," Moon said. "The food wasn't bad, either."

One guy in Moon's group, Ralf Traugott, was a car dealer from Boston, and he was a big hit with the Amal. Moon said they liked his macho style and his love for partying. They took him out with them to a disco one night and did Beirut after dark. Traugott said he witnessed a strange sight indeed. It was 3:00 A.M., and right through the middle of Beirut came a funeral procession, led by a tank.

We settled down with Moon's group, exchanging hostage stories and happy to see that we were all in reasonably good shape. Since we were being grouped into larger units, it seemed reasonable to assume they were preparing to free us. At least we kept our hopes up.

Two hostages from San Francisco and Ralf settled down to play cards with the guards. It turned out the "Eat the Rich" guard was a nice enough guy after all.

Then, at about 11:00 P.M., more guards appeared and told us we were going out to dinner.

Now it was thirteen of us who had to jam into the VW bus. Off we went into the night. The guards seemed nervous. Amal guards drove in front and back of us, with guns blazing in the air to clear the intersections.

"I know where we're going," Dr. Moon said. Sure enough, about two minutes later we screeched to a halt in front of the Miami Beach Restaurant. "It's closed again," Moon said. A couple of Amal guards went to bang on the door of the owners' upstairs apartment. But they weren't home. That really botched their plans, because by now all sorts of other vehicles were arriving, some containing Amal militiamen, some containing other hostages. Here were all the hijacked Americans, the Amal guards, and a closed restaurant.

After discussing things for a few minutes, pointing this way and that, the guards got back into their vehicles.

Our late-night dinner convoy continued, and it was hard to see where we were headed because the guards wanted us to keep our heads down. I'd sneak glances from time to time, and, looking back, it appeared that there were other vehicles in the convoy, which I had not noticed before. Perhaps all the hostages are being taken around with us, I thought.

Every time our convoy met a strange car, our guards would fire warning shots from a .50-caliber gun mounted on the top of a land cruiser, then stop and check out the occupants of the vehicle.

It became obvious that they were giving up on the local eateries, and we headed for Beirut's suburbs. Abruptly, the bomb-ripped city gave way to an unscathed area of nice homes and buildings. There must be an agreement not to bomb this part of town, I thought.

I found out why—nobody wants to destroy the place we pulled up to.

The Summerland Resort is the plushest of the resorts that used to dot the Lebanese coast. Most of the resorts have fallen victim to the wars, but not this one. It has three swimming pools and a thousand deck chairs. If you prefer salt water, it has its own beach and a marina. There's a health club and sauna. The place has its own power system to cope with the faulty Beirut electric company's frequent breakdowns. There are white-coated waiters, trendy boutiques, several restaurants. Not a bullet hole anywhere I could see.

We were about to find out that an international news event was being created—totally by accident. Around the world, breathless reporters would file stories about the Amal's banquet for the hostages at the Summerland Resort.

I don't know if the Amal leadership was aware of where we were, but I don't think our drivers knew that virtually all the Western TV and newspaper reporters had been holed up in the Summerland during the hostage crisis, waiting for a break in the story.

Now here we were, being escorted into their midst for dinner— and they figured it was all planned that way.

Apparently they'd never been down to the Miami Beach Restaurant.

ABC television crews were the first to see us. They were flabbergasted as we walked into the courtyard, and they scrambled over each other to grab cameras and plug in wires and bulky cables. Get ready, New York: have we got a story for you.

It was after midnight, and the Summerland's restaurants were closed for the night, but our guards had rousted the cooks out of bed to make us a meal.

One fellow from ABC talked with us at length and took down messages he said he'd send to our families in the States. He seemed genuinely concerned for us and didn't attempt any hard interviewing. ABC wanted to get us all on camera, especially those who hadn't been seen on television before, so our families would be reassured.

The cooks began scurrying around the kitchens, and the first thing they did was bring us Cokes, any kind of drink we wanted—nonalcoholic, though; the Amal frown on liquor.

We sat around the pool, overlooking the ocean. What a beautiful sight in the middle of a war zone. The waves were breaking on the beach, and I could see fish jumping in the moonlight. A balmy breeze was blowing in from the sea. Just beautiful. It felt good to breathe fresh air again.

Then the waiters began to deliver tray after tray of scrumptious food—steaks, chicken, vegetables, french fries; it seemed like an endless supply.

But I couldn't partake of the Beirut "all you can eat" buffet. I was really sick to my stomach, and food was not what I had on my mind.

Three things were on my mind: I wanted to get my face on TV so my family could see I was still breathing. I wanted to continue enjoying the marvelous night air. And I wanted to use the toilet.

In fact, my fondest memory of the Summerland is the sit-down toilet. A real toilet, with a roll of toilet paper at my side. Most wonderful. I had guards standing outside the door, but no matter.

Those Summerland cooks were amazing. They managed to whip up a giant sheetcake, saying, "Welcome Home Hostages," or "Have a Safe Journey Home." I can't quite remember which, but it was something along those lines. I think that's where the media got the idea this was a farewell banquet.

In addition to being interviewed by ABC, some of the hostages were getting to make telephone calls home, and I was anxiously awaiting my chance. But it was not to be.

The Summerland's chefs had just wheeled out the cake when,

from a distance, we heard a commotion. The other media people had gotten wind of ABC's scoop and had all stumbled out of bed and into battle mode. Here were all these crazy media guys, running, shouting, and flashing cameras as they charged into the resort.

They were an imposing force, and the Amal guards got scared. I didn't blame them. The media people blew our cover, and the Amal quickly gathered us together, the thirty-two hostages in the dinner party, and whisked us away, back to the apartment with Dr. Moon's party.

I slept fairly well, but awoke before everyone else and washed up. At 8:30 I turned on the radio for the BBC morning news. A formal statement had been signed between the U.S. and Syria, and we would be taken to Damascus and turned over to U.S. authorities. We would be in Damascus sometime early in the afternoon.

"Well, all right!" I shouted and awakened my fellow hostages. "We're going home!"

20
Freedom

At 9:30 Saturday, they loaded us into the VW bus to take us back to the schoolyard where we had met with the Red Cross, in the Burj al Barajneh section of Beirut, a ramshackle Shi'ite neighborhood.

As we drove through the morning air, past checkpoints and down bombed-out side streets, I explained further the nature of the deal that had been made for our release. The other hostages had considered me somewhat of an expert on the politics of the situation. Actually, I had no special knowledge; I just listened constantly to the BBC and had been doing so since we first got the radio, in the early days of our captivity.

"The Reagan administration is denying the reported deal," I said. "But I think they leaked the details on purpose, as often happens in these kinds of things. The Syrians are the ones with the real clout.

"We get sprung, and Israel will release something like 735 Shi'ite hostages they are still holding, people who the BBC says have not been charged with any crimes. But Israel will not admit that the release has anything to do with our situation. Everyone has to save face."

"That's OK, just so long as we get out of here," someone piped up from the back of the bus.

We were soon back in the schoolyard. Other hostage groups were arriving, and Allyn Conwell. He had met with Nabih Berri. Allyn took us over to the CNN reporters, and he started reading off the list of hostage names.

Bad news. Four people didn't answer—the four being held by the Hizbollah. They would be here soon, we were told. We would not leave without them.

I met a reporter from a Beirut newspaper. It wasn't easy being a journalist in Beirut, he said. No, censorship wasn't a problem. In Beirut there is a more primitive but effective way of dealing with reporters who write unflattering stories. The reporter pulled up his pants leg to reveal a mass of scar tissue below the knee.

"They don't kill you, just shoot you in the leg," he shrugged. He said he had been shot like that seventeen times.

I heard a smattering of applause from some of the hostages, and there was the flight crew, looking tired but with cleanly pressed uniforms. I went over to Captain Testrake, who was being besieged by other hostages and television reporters.

"Hi, I'm Kurt Carlson."

"Captain Testrake, your pilot," came the reply. He went on shaking hands—obviously, he didn't remember I was the guy getting beat up just behind his seat on the airplane.

I walked over to Phil, the copilot, and said, "I was the man beaten in Algiers."

"Oh, my God," he said. "Let's go and talk with John. I know he'll want to talk with you."

Phil told me the hijackers had instructed the crew never to turn their heads to the back, or they would be hit over the head. They also were told to keep their headphones on. So they never got a look at me and heard very little.

When Phil went up to Testrake and whispered something in his ear, he excused himself from the hubbub and came over to talk with us. "I'm sorry, I couldn't recognize you because I never got a look," Testrake said.

We talked about the first few hours of the hijacking. Testrake said he was frustrated with the U.S. government because, although they knew the hijacking was taking place, they never gave any instructions to him.

Phil had his own ideas as to how to quash the hijacking, but Testrake wouldn't permit him to carry them out. Phil wanted to push one hijacker out the cockpit window in Algiers, then gang up on the other one. "But we turned around, and the other guy had a .45 and a hand grenade, so we held back," Phil said.

Then, on the second trip to Beirut, after we were off the plane, Testrake said Phil wanted him to collapse the landing gear. Too dangerous, the pilot told him. Then Phil wanted to slide the plane off the runway, immobilizing it. Testrake vetoed that, too. The hijackers were too crazy, he'd told Phil; they could panic and blow the plane up. John Testrake was a strong leader and had made the right decisions.

We milled around that schoolyard for twelve hours. The International Red Cross people were there: a doctor and a spokesman, and six drivers. All of them were Swiss.

Incredibly, the BBC, which had been our rock throughout the crisis as far as dependable news went, was way off the mark this morning. We stood around listening to a noon report that we were on the road to Damascus. At 2:00 P.M., the radio said we'd crossed the Syrian border. We only wished the BBC was right.

We knew now a hitch had developed that was not planned by Nabih Berri and the Amal. Apparently the Hizbollah faction decided that Berri did not have an ironclad guarantee that there would be no retaliation by the Sixth Fleet.

There was speculation that Reagan's tough talk the day before might have scuttled our release. Reagan had said at a rally in Chicago Heights that the hijackers were "murderers, thugs, and thieves." He said there was no linkage between Israeli plans to release the Atlit prisoners and the release of the Flight 847 hostages. He seemed to warn of reprisals against the hijackers and their sponsors. "I don't think anything that attempts to get people back who have been kidnapped by thugs, murderers, and barbarians is wrong to do."

The U.S. press was screaming that the rhetoric had scuttled the release and that the Hizbollah, widely believed to have planned and carried out the hijacking, were scared of air strikes and other retaliation.

But my new Beirut journalist friend had another theory. "Berri was extremely embarrassed by the Hizbollah's refusal to release their hostages. Understand that the Hizbollah don't trust Berri. They believe he is too westernized, not religious, too friendly with Americans."

"Makes sense," I replied, thinking of Berri's children and ex-wife living near Detroit.

"Mr. Reagan's remarks pleased Berri, because it made him appear to be another victim of American saber-rattling. What the remarks did was buy him time to deal with the Hizbollah."

Berri responded to Reagan with his own rhetoric, demanding that the U.S. guarantee no retaliation against Lebanon.

The U.S. dusted off an old diplomatic position, saying it respects the sovereignty of Lebanon, its people, and hopes for "the mitigation of the suffering of its people."

The journalist, and I, too, wondered if the whole series of events between Berri and the Reagan administration had been orchestrated for the benefit of the Hizbollah. I still wonder.

Negotiations took place on a lower level, too. I saw an Amal colonel pacing back and forth with a Hizbollah *mullah*, or priest, who was the communications link with the people holding the four hostages. I felt that the Hizbollah had to prove to their people that they were not just Amal puppets.

So, it took a while to preserve everyone's manhood, I guess. Anyway, we were getting bored and tired in the schoolyard.

Cable News Network interviewed some of us. Stuart talked of Stethem. "He was my friend," Stuart said sadly. "We thought we were done for, but [the Amal] treated us real kind. They brought us to a different place and fed us, and for a while the terror was over anyway. We decided we were probably better off. I think the Amal militia really saved our lives by pulling us off the plane."

Tony Watson said hello to his wife and kids back in Virginia. "I've been treated very well. It was a little scary at first."

Ralf Traugott, the Massachusetts car dealer who'd partied with the Amal guards, said he was confused about Beirut and U.S. policy in this part of the world. "I don't know enough about politics," he said.

I kept thinking about what would happen if the Hizbollah hostages didn't show up. Would they release the rest of us? The Reagan administration was saying it was "all or none." I thought that maybe Berri's men couldn't find the other four hostages.

I approached Ali Hamdan, the Amal public relations man, about it. "No, the four have not been moved, and we know exactly where they are. We are working to get them out and satisfy the Hizbollah, too. It is difficult, but don't worry."

We waited until 10:00 P.M. Saturday. We were exhausted, and the Amal leaders, with frustrated, embarrassed expressions, led us off into waiting cars and vans. They had been humiliated on live, international television, and they knew it.

We weren't going to Damascus. My group was taken up the mountain to an expensive-looking high rise owned by an attorney. His brother was an Amal leader, killed by Israelis, we were told.

We were given a vacant, fifth-floor apartment. We were treated very graciously by the lawyer, who showed us a picture of his brother hanging on the wall.

The attorney had a videocassette recorder, and we finally got to watch *Dog Day Afternoon*, which was what we'd just been through. We also saw *Mutiny on the Bounty*. I thought Nabih Berri must have felt like Captain Bligh about now, with the Hizbollah mutineers scuttling his deal. Two Amal guards stayed with us.

The attorney didn't speak English but made it clear he wanted us to make ourselves at home. His seven-year-old son demonstrated his skill at handling one of the guards' AK-47s.

I got to sleep in a real bed for the first time since we had been hijacked.

We slept in on Sunday. At about 11:00, they came for us again and took us back to the schoolyard. The four missing hostages were there. We broke into a cheer, rejoicing that we were finally all together and going home.

But not until Ali Hamdan earned his pay as the Amal's public relations man. He had a farewell speech prepared and written out.

"We, the Shia Amal under the leadership of Mr. Nabih Berri, rescued you from the hijackers and protected you during the subsequent negotiations," he said.

"We had to hold you until the Israelis agreed to release their hostages, because we gave our word to the hijackers as a condition for your release into our safe custody."

We were piling into white cars with bright red crosses on the sides when Ali handed me an envelope with my name on it.

"A message from your family," he said. "The night of the banquet, your telephone call went through after you had gone."

An ABC television reporter had taken the call and written down a brief message from my mom. "We love you," it said. "The whole family is praying for your safe return. Cheri is now born again."

Tears filled my eyes as we loaded into the convoy of cars and pulled out. The Swiss doctor drove our vehicle.

And now began an experience that was at once unexpected, confusing, sad, and terrifying. We began slowly winding our way through West Beirut, past scenes of more devastation, which reminded me of pictures of European cities in World War II. To the front and rear of our convoy were the Amal militia in their trucks, with the .50-caliber guns mounted on top. They were still fearful of a Hizbollah ambush.

We entered the run-down Shi'ite neighborhoods of the city, and the strangest thing happened—we certainly could not explain it.

The residents had lined the streets and were waving from balconies, cheering at us, jumping up and down. We felt like Neil Armstrong, just returned from the moon. It was that kind of emotion.

People ran up to our cars, handing in flowers, boxes of candy, bottles of wine. What had we done to deserve this?

The Swiss doctor gave a knowing smile and attempted an answer. "You took the brunt of the pain so their people being held in Israel will be released. Their relatives will be coming home, so they bid you welcome, too. They see you as heroes. Relax and enjoy it."

We enjoyed it, but the Amal guards certainly did not. They were nervous, looking off in all directions, fearful of an angry sniper, or a man lobbing a grenade, or any number of things. The Amal had issued an order forbidding the discharge of weapons. Usually the Lebanese shoot guns in the air during celebrations like this. We were glad they didn't this time.

The drive to Damascus was over some dangerous territory. The road was indescribable: a bumpy, bomb-cratered, beat-up black-top. It's only about seventy miles or so, but it was a five-hour drive. We wound out of the city, out of the Shi'ite area, into a section inhabited by Druse Muslims. Here I noticed bulldozers and road-graders fixing the road and nearby streets.

That made sense, I thought, because Walid Jumblatt, the Druse leader, is minister of public works. Thinking back to Chicago and tales of Mayor Daley, I remembered, "He who fixes the streets has the real clout." I filed that thought away for future reference, in case I ever hear of a coup attempt in which Druse militiamen, armed with Caterpillars and giant dump trucks, seize the presidential palace.

The doctor plugged a tape into the Peugeot's radio, and I noticed that it was loose in its mountings.

"Somebody tried to steal the radio during the night at the schoolyard," he said. "But either he got scared off or they caught him before he could get it out."

We plugged on, bumping along the road, out of the Druse sector and into the Bekaa Valley, home of the Hizbollah. All but one group of Amal guards left us, and we were now to be escorted by Syrian soldiers. They were not ragtags like the Amal, but very professional, with cleanly pressed uniforms, red camouflage, and red berets, sort of like the Lebanese Army soldiers we had seen at the airport.

The Hizbollah had been told to stay in their houses. But they'd ignored the Syrians' orders, and now they, too, lined the road. However, they didn't see us as heroes. They stood either silently or clenching fists. The women were covered from head to toe in the traditional Shi'ite black robes, with only their eyes visible. From modern Beirut, we had entered another century, perhaps the fifteenth. The American consul, who traveled with the convoy, said he'd never seen the Hizbollah demonstrate in such a way. He thought we were going to have an incident. The tension continued for about twenty minutes, and we counted every second nervously. The Syrians fired their weapons into the air as a warning—they weren't putting up with any monkey business that would make President Hassad look bad. He was touting his role as the deal maker, after all. If these troops didn't deliver us to Damascus alive, Hassad may have to answer to someone—maybe someone in Moscow.

When we left Hizbollahland, we entered Syria, and the road changed to a smooth, four-lane blacktop. We sped up and relaxed a bit, figuring Hassad wouldn't allow any ominous roadside types to mar the rest of our journey.

All at once, a bright light flashed in our car's rearview mirror. Oh no, I thought. The Road Warrior! But, getting a closer look, I saw this intrepid television cameraman, leaning halfway out the van's window, shooting us, all right—with videotape. It was Beirut TV, come to get some footage to wedge between "Dallas" and "Magnum P.I."

I looked ahead. There was an abutment—the Beirut eyewitness news team was about to hit it at high speed. Their brakes locked, and the car swerved, just missing the barrier, and plunged into the desert, kicking up clouds of dust and sand.

I thought we'd lost them, but, no, five minutes later, they roared up again, shone their light, and shot tape. Anything for a story.

We arrived at the Damascus Sheraton, entered the lobby, and met the U.S. ambassador, who said he'd just returned from a vacation. We were escorted into a lounge area, where drinks and hors d' oeuvres were served. We were introduced to an American woman, the assistant ambassador or something, who, we were told, had negotiated with Syria to help secure our release.

We had another news conference. Very dignified, calm, and controlled. The Syrians were more sophisticated at media manipulation than the Amal. They were organized.

Then it was outside, into buses for the ride to the airport. Our anticipation was growing, our adrenaline pumping faster and faster. The ride took only about ten minutes, but it seemed like an eternity.

Then, as we wheeled around the airport driveway, there she was, the most beautiful sight—except for Meredith—I have ever seen in my life. A giant, camouflaged C-141 sitting on the tarmac, waiting to take us away.

We drove through an airfield security gate and directly up to the airplane. Two U.S. Army medical officers boarded our bus.

"Our whole country is awaiting your return," they said. "Our team will fly you the first leg of your journey home.

"We'll give you more instructions after we're airborne. By the way, I don't want to alarm anyone, but the Syrians did not send us a power unit to start the airplane's engines."

He said they had requested the unit several times, with no response. The Syrians didn't know that the C-141's engines can be hand-cranked like a Model-A Ford. The crew and the medical team had actually jump-started the plane.

"We have your baggage on the ground," the medical officer said, "but we can't load it without checking for bombs. So we recommend leaving it here. It'll follow us on a commercial flight tomorrow."

I'd thought the ordeal had ended, but the pressure was still on. I wouldn't feel safe until the bird lifted off.

We scurried up the loading ramp into the plane's belly and sat down in the airline-style seats installed in the cargo hold.

The plane began its taxi to the runway even as the ramp was still closing. The pilot came on the intercom.

"The sky around us looks clear, and we are going to head for the runway and call the tower."

A couple of minutes later, the pilot said the tower gave us clearance to take off.

"And they are now sending out the generator truck," he noted wryly, as we laughed.

I settled back in my seat, and as the plane lumbered down the runway and into the air, we let out a loud cheer.

We were on our way home.

Amen.

Epilogue:
Out of the Vortex

Thoughts of fear and survival began changing to feelings of freedom and happiness as the C-141 winged out of Damascus for the six-hour flight to Germany.

I thought of my wife Cheri and baby Meredith and tried to forget the long days of terror. I was open to the beautiful faces and kindness of our new escorts, the U.S. Air Force crew and the army medical team.

For an hour, I sat up front in the cockpit with the flight crew, just looking at the stars and listening to the radio communications. For the first time in many days, I was at ease.

I heard Air Force 2 call in and say they would be landing at Rhein-Main Air Base just ahead of us and that Vice President Bush would come aboard to greet us personally.

The BBC had often broadcast Bush's comments, along with those of the president, during our ordeal. From the beginning, I had had faith in our government leaders, and I believe they came through for us.

I best remember the president's statement that our safe return was the first priority of our government. I believe his show of strength and threats of retaliation with the Sixth Fleet were heard and respected by the Lebanese. Even the Hizbollah will listen to someone with a bigger gun. The moderate Lebanese Shia were more frightened by the president's threat of an economic blockade. Without their Marlboros, Pepsi, and videos, the Lebanese people might finally revolt and throw out the warlords and militiamen.

The volume of news coverage of the incident gave the whole world a long look at the Middle East and its problems, and, by keeping attention riveted on our plight, the press may well have kept us alive.

U.S. opinion pressured the Israeli government to release Lebanese hostages. The Syrians gained prestige in negotiating with the Shia for our freedom. We, the thirty-nine American hostages, were caught in the middle of an international diplomatic crisis, and we were released only after everyone had his say. In the eyes of the Lebanese as well as our own countrymen, we were all heroes. If so, we were most certainly unwilling heroes.

I wanted to put this whole episode behind me, and as Joe, the Amal commander, had said, "just have thoughts about home and family."

But I learned that would be impossible.

First of all, I discovered I couldn't go anywhere in my hometown without being treated like a hero. I'd pull into a gas station and get hugged by someone who recognized me. People stopped me in restaurants and said they'd prayed for me. I was overwhelmed at the outpouring of warmth.

I'd been back only two days when the town had me suit up in my uniform and ride atop a convertible in the Fourth of July parade.

I remember watching myself on TV news that night.

"What did you like most about the parade, the floats or bands?" a pretty reporter asked a young child.

"I liked Kurt Carlson the best," the kid said.

Life was going to be different.

Everyone wanted to know about my ordeal. Speaking requests poured in; they still do.

So I give my talk, combining the fear with the ridiculous. They laugh about Hassan and Pistol, and Beirut television. They fall silent when I speak of the terror.

I give the talks not only to satisfy people's curiosity, but also to make some kind of statement, in my way, about what I think got me out of that place.

Just simple faith. I always thought the God I believed in would get me out of there. If I was supposed to live, I would. And I did.

The sadness, of course, is that the same God allowed Bob Stethem to die. Why, I can't judge. I'm no philosopher; I'm a roofing contractor.

But I do know the one reality of that flight was that "one American must die." The hijacker kept repeating it, as if it was part of a master plan.

And as Stuart said in our cell, Bob had a faith stronger than the rest of us. Perhaps he was the one most ready to die.

I know that for a time I thought I was the one to die. On the floor of that airplane, crumpled in pain, I was sure I had just ten minutes to live.

I am surprised at what came into my mind.

They say your life flashes before you.

Well, what flashed through my head was a very selective group of thoughts. Not about my business or my achievements. Nothing about possessions or specific places I'd been.

My thoughts were only of people: family members; friends, old and new. Good times we'd had together. And the thoughts made me not afraid to die. I wasn't going out of life in terror or fear; these people were somehow with me. So it was love that was important when push came to shove.

And since I've been home, I've found myself spending more time with those people, making the time, even at the expense of "more important" matters.

People are the only important matters. Family. Good friends.

Old friends. I must have called all my old buddies since I've been back. Guys I hadn't had time to see in years.

New friends. I talked for hours with Uli on the phone. She cried because she thought I was dead on that plane. I told her I thought I was, too. She wants to keep in touch.

And my cellmates—Stuart, Clint, Ken, Tony. We've a bond that nothing can break. We plan to have reunions whenever we can, to learn how we're all doing, and to get to know each others' families.

I'm always amused, now that I'm Kurt Carlson, former hostage, that people assume I'm an expert with ready solutions to the problems of the Middle East.

The only solution is to take away all the guns. But then I remember my history: they've been using that part of the world as a battlefield since back when all they had to throw at each other was rocks.

What I think about daily are the children. That's one thing I noticed about the Lebanese: they love their children; they're devoted to them. I wonder bitterly how many of them got blown up last month and how many will be pressed into some militia at ten or twelve, as Pistol was.

The day we left, in fact, the Amal attacked the Druse. A few weeks later, they were at it with the Palestinians. And on and on.

I guess I needed to tell this story, if only to warn people about what life is like in a place where nobody talks and everybody shoots.

It's a place you don't want to be.